Be the Beacon

A Ladies Power Lunch

Transformation Anthology

Be the light to others! Your confidence will lead the way! Mary

Dr. Davia H. Shepherd & Elizabeth B. Hill, MSW

with

*Kristi Borst, Mary Campbell, Mary Carangelo, Robin Finney,
Anne Garland, Adria D. Giordano, Aina L. Hoskins,
Wendy Lee, Michelle R. Lemoi, Laura Monk, Jess Paré,
Barb Pritchard, Lori Raggio, Akanke Rasheed,
Velanda Samuel, Debbie Sodergren, and Tashella K. Smith*

Green Heart Living Press

Be the Beacon

ISBN (paperback): 978-1-954493-17-9

Cover design: Barb Pritchard

Dedication

To all the beacons of light and love who are ready to share their light with us all.

Together, we raise the vibration of our planet.

Table of Contents

Dear Reader,

You may have lost your spark.

You may be hiding your light under a bushel.

You may spend your days helping others find their spark, nurturing them to a growing flame.

You may have been handed a torch, but it feels too hot to hold. It burns the skin.

You may be on a dark path. You may not be able to see your own light.

You may have felt the inner spark expand into a wild bonfire.

You may have walked through the fire. You may have found healing in its flames.

You may be in the healing fire now. It might not feel so healing.

Wherever you are, you will find your life, your light, reflected here. As a moon reflects the beauty of the sun, our authors will reflect the beauty of your life and your story. Even if you can't quite see it for yourself now.

Love & Transformation,

Elizabeth

Introduction

Dr. Davia Shepherd

CHO Ladies' Power Lunch

If this is the first of the Ladies Power Lunch (LPL) Anthologies that you have picked up, I welcome you. If you have connected with our LPL collaborative writing projects in the past, welcome back!

I wear a lot of hats, just like you. I'm a mom, a sister, a daughter, and a wife. I help my patients feel better every day, but the one thing that I'm most passionate about, the one thing that gets me out of bed in the mornings and into the office on a Monday, is the opportunity to support women in business to live their optimal lives. I do this by helping them to grow their visibility, their reach, their impact, and their income. I'm a beacon for beacons... but it's more than that.

I'm an amplifier. I have combined almost two decades of experience in corporate as well as running my own community practice, with my innate ability to translate the energetic signature of the best version of you into words. You know that big dream that you didn't even know you had, for both your business and your life? Step into my field and I can not only translate it, but also make it bigger.

I take that higher vision of you and use it to develop a solid plan for increased visibility, reach, and success. The result is that you shine your light at its most brilliant. You stop being the world's best kept secret. Your optimal clients, the ones that are losing sleep at night because they need you, the ones who light up when you work together, they are then able to find you with ease and grace, and you can BE THE BEACON that your potential suggests.

Our Ladies Power Lunch group started from humble beginnings. I had just started out in private practice and was disillusioned with the traditional ways that people suggested for accepting new patients/clients, and so I invited a group of six heart-centered women in business to have lunch with me at a Ruby Tuesday on Route 6 in Bristol, Connecticut. When women get together something magical happens. They tap into a wisdom that we have known for millennia and they support each other, not just because they expect to get something in return but because they are women, they are there, and they can. At the table on that first day it was a true power lunch! Connections were made, support was given, we laughed, we cried and then we decided that this had to be a part of our lives going forward. It was just too valuable to be a one off. That was eight years ago. Now, we boast an organic membership that spans continents. That's the power of women. We have moved beyond being just a women's group and we have morphed into a movement. A movement of women, and a few amazing men, who have just one simple rule: We support each other in an intentional and aligned way.

Over the years one thing has stood out to me about the members of our Ladies' Power Lunch movement. The kind of people who are drawn to being in service of growing each other's businesses are the kind of people who are here to make a difference in the world. They are the kind of people who whatever they are doing as their profession, they are doing it in service of the greater good. They know that they are beacons and that in whatever capacity they are here to serve they are here to shine their light into the world and play their part in raising the vibration of the planet.

Another thing I have noticed is that many of our members are tremendously skilled at what they do, but they also may be the world's best kept secret. The people that are losing sleep at night needing the services that they provide by sharing their passion, well, those amazing folks can't find them. This causes a ripple effect: their potential client's lights can't shine as brightly, they can't influence the people they were meant to serve in the way they were meant to... and on and on it goes, inception style.

What a conundrum! I sat with this for a while, meditated on it and asked Source, as it has been my more recent practice, and the answer that came through for me is that I needed to do what I do best. I needed to be the beacon for the beacons. I needed to amplify their light so that they have a platform for greater visibility. Ever the recovering researcher, I looked a little more deeply into how we could achieve our goal of being the beacon for the beacons and the four paths were laid out for me as clear as day. Tremendous synchronicities showed up. Members of our LPL group showed up to support our project and before we knew it we had a program available to help our amazing members be seen and to help the voices of light be heard around the globe. You will agree, this is so necessary especially now.

So what are the four pillars of visibility? The first thing to consider is COLLABORATION. If you know me at all, hardly a sentence passes my lips without the word collaboration being included. I like to joke that I love collaboration so much that I even wrote a whole book about it. In this day and age of email lists and social media, most entrepreneurs have at least 3-4,000 connections. If we get together a group of 20 like-minded souls with aligned intention, suddenly, the combined reach of such a group with room for overlap expands our reach to over 50,000. That's why we start with collaboration. Building a truly meaningful heart-centered community among folks with one beautiful aim: raising the collective vibration.

The next pillar that Source pointed me to: SPEAKING. We already had the framework for opportunities to speak with our LPL monthly meetings, summits and retreats PLUS our network of LPL members, who host all manner of events, and are always looking for speakers. We also tapped into the wisdom of our speaker trainers in the group who are here to guide our members to speak more eloquently and authentically in an engaging manner about their passion and learn the business of getting booked on the right stages.

When Source showed me PODCASTING as the third pillar of visibility, I laughed out loud! "Look at Source being all tech savvy and what not," I thought. I think Source had a nice chuckle as well before pointing out to me that podcasting is the media form that is growing right now, and that while starting their own podcast might not be what is necessary for our beacons, being able to be guests on podcasts that we can connect them with and being guest hosts of the LPL podcast can bring the visibility in this digital format that no other media can compete with. Of course if you need anything, all you need to do is check within our LPL community. Our member who is a media expert and podcast producer Jim Williams stepped in to support our members in that way.

Our fourth pillar of visibility is PUBLISHING. One of the best ways to become recognized as the leader the world needs now, is by becoming a bestselling author. Our LPL member Elizabeth Hill of Green Heart Living Press stepped in to support our members on their journey to tell their beacon stories. These are the stories that we are sharing with you here in the LPL Transformation Anthology series. All of our LPL Transformation Anthologies are best-sellers multiple times over, including the one that you have your hands on today.

I consulted with my business shaman Veronica Wirth about what else I needed and her spirit guides pointed me in the direction of tying it all together with savvy marketing, branding and design and our LPL member Barb Prichard stepped in and filled that void adding beautiful WebPages, graphics, book covers, sizzle reels and production assistance.

Along our journey to birthing this beautiful meaningful book about beacons for beacons, so many members of the LPL community contributed, all of whom cannot be named here, or this book would end up being just a 500 page list of amazing individuals, but if you want to meet the peeps, just join our free LPL community we welcome you.

In this *Be The Beacon* anthology, we invite you to use these stories as an opportunity and a reminder to shine your light at its brightest. We discover that beacons come in all shapes and sizes and can be described in a few categories. The underlying theme here is that no matter what your beacon looks like, tending your beacon and amplifying your beacon have to be the most important goals in life. In doing those two things, everything else falls into place.

In this book you will read stories about the beacons who are ***Sparks (Discovering Our Light.)*** These beacons demonstrate that when a spark meets a flammable material, in no time both are set ablaze. If reading their stories resonates with you, my reminder to you is: Your purpose in life is to be an instigator, a change maker, a beacon to success for others. You're naturally innovative. You may be just starting out or you may be taking your passion/beacon into new and amazing heights that may challenge you a little. You find new, unexpected solutions to old problems. The world needs leaders like you to shine forth, now more than ever.

In this anthology, you will come across stories of beacons that I identify as Bonfires. You might identify with this beautiful beacon if you have healed by going through the fire and coming through on the other side as the proverbial Phoenix. Or you might have come to your beacon status through your search for home, hearth, and belonging. Either way you are here to be the roaring blaze that the visual of a bonfire evokes. These beacons share their stories in the sections ***Ignite (Healing through Fire)*** and ***Hearth (Finding Home, Finding Our Light.)***

If you are feeling like the idea of being a BONFIRE beacon speaks to you then you already know that you are the type of person that people naturally listen to when you speak. Your effortless optimism inspires others to seek the light in dark circumstances. Being a bonfire means that you are leading even when you aren't trying; Just shining your light and being an outstanding example allows others who see you to be encouraged to shine their beautiful light as well.

And, of course, we have those of you who identify as the

lighthouse ***Beacon (Lighting the Path.)***

My favorite thing about the lighthouse is that your ego is firmly checked at the door. You know without a shadow of a doubt that shining your light brighter and bigger does not diminish the light of another, it only shows her how bright her light has the potential to shine. You are embracing the idea that you, yes you, are a teacher, influencer, leader, guru, mentor or wise woman (or man.) Your job, should you choose to accept it, involves linking arms with other humans just like you, who know that they are here to BE THE BEACON of light, hope, love, and support that the world needs now.

Calling all BEACONS! I invite YOU to join our LPL movement. Let us all shine our beautiful lights and let's do it together! Learn more about us at ladiespowerlunch.com.

Selah

Spark

Discovering Our Light

Mary Campbell

"We were born with the spark of joy alight within us. It bursts to flame when we strike the match of feminine delight to the tinder of our healthy masculine intention."

Velanda Samuel, MSW, LCSW

"I learned that whatever I needed or wanted to achieve it had to come from God and from the strength that I had within me. "

Kristi Borst, PhD

"In Truth, we are here because we each hold a unique radiance of light and love. We recognize that spark easily in newborns and infants. It's time to re-ignite your spark!"

Akanke Rasheed

"I became more open to express myself, to get in touch with my passions, desires, and overall curiosity about life—particularly my life and what I could become if I had more faith in myself, "The Universe," and unknown possibilities."

Mary Carangelo

"Lead with confidence and beauty will follow."

Barb Pritchard

"If you can see it, you believe it. If you believe it, you become it."

Chapter 1

From Doing to Being

Mary Campbell

Most women are so busy doing life that we have no time or space to be the light we were designed to enjoy. We're just too distracted or exhausted to notice it.

When we lose ourselves in the doing, we lose our access to joy and our inner light. To be able to experience that light, that joy, we need a healthy balance of masculine and feminine energies in our life.

Trouble is, we weren't taught how to enjoy this moment-to-moment life, to naturally relax and receive all that's here waiting to delight us.

I know I wasn't.

I was taught to get things done.

And it's little wonder. Doing, rather than enjoying being, was what brought praise. We live in societies constructed to prioritize the values of those who were the esteemed winners, and they were most often men. No matter our gender, setting high goals and meeting them is how we learned to win.

I'd grown up learning how to win my parents' love and approval. The oldest of five and "mother's little helper," I learned to do what brought praise and hide anything that didn't. The threat of punishment beat me into a people-pleasing perfectionist, obedient and afraid to try anything I wasn't assured of winning. I sang solos in the choir, won blue ribbons at the county fair, and went off to college on scholarship, graduating valedictorian of my class. A lot of doing to win what promised to bring happiness!

Modeling how women traditionally won in Western Pennsylvania in the early 70's, my carefully crafted attentiveness attracted cute boyfriends and in short order, a promising husband. I loved the new feeling of connection and intimacy in my body and heart that made any personal sacrifices to autonomy easier to tolerate, at least for a while.

Becoming a school teacher, I combined my delight in human connection with an avenue for success and praise. But striving to be the best motivated me to work harder than ever to excel, writing lesson plans into the evening and for hours every weekend. I thrived on winning my principal's praise, the children's affections, and my own sense of achievement, but my perpetual overworking eventually diminished the joy I'd found in teaching.

While my choices, like most women's roles for thousands of years, were proscribed and limited by tradition and a lack of options, the 60's mass migration of women to traditionally male jobs finally offered women the opportunity for creative expression, autonomy, and financial success as never before possible, at least in recorded history. Women delighted in their successes, relishing the pure joy of exploring their unique talents and capacities. They made their own money, built their own businesses, and lived the aspirations their foremothers could only dream of.

Never have women experienced such huge advances in so short a time. But in pushing so hard for success out in the man's world, those of us who identified as female too often lost touch with a feminine balance that could bring the joy we most wanted. I work with women who've devoted themselves to a career and the success they thought would make them happy, but now regret what they fear they've lost for good. "Where's the happiness I thought all of this would bring?" they ask.

The masculine paradigm of earning success in the most efficient and effective ways possible, no matter the cost in personal, human, and planetary suffering, has been rewarded by those in power for thousands of years. Values more commonly attributed to women such as gentleness, compassion and emotional/intuitive knowing were considered weak and unimportant, often mocked, devalued and despised by those whose physical and societal power could win through domination and power-over politics (Eisler, *The Chalice and the Blade*, 1987).

Lest you think I'm here to beat up on men, let me clarify my use of particular words and their meanings. Please don't be confused by my use of the terms *masculine* and *feminine*. I use these words to refer to energies, not genders. All genders possess both expressions, to a greater or lesser extent depending on their genetics, conditioning, and culture. Unfortunately most societies have traditionally ascribed certain expressions to specific genders, causing untold damage and misfortune.

Masculine energy, sometimes referred to as *yang* in Taoist traditions, carries a strength and integrity that is often quiet, but substantial. A humble and competent stillness in the face of danger. Able to take a joke and smile at their humanity.

Its presence speaks for itself. And when it does, every bone in your body resonates to its bass note of truth. The healthy masculine feels solid, trustworthy. It's strong, but never forced; exacting but not self-serving. It harnesses its power for the greater good. It's decisive, consistent, and determined, but never a bully. You feel its confidence, without bravado.

Healthy masculine energy has no need for a big show of strength because its logical positions are founded in what can be proven by observation or science. It is strategic and fierce when protecting those in need. It knows how to maintain a firm and safe container, structuring life so the feminine can relax and blossom.

This is the masculine I long to recognize and celebrate in others. It's also what I want to develop in myself to undergird my actions as I stand for what's most healthy for my world, as well as myself.

Feminine energy expresses itself through connection and care; the masculine ensures essential safety and security creating the structure and organization to get things done. Our feminine energy brings the enjoyment of what life can be. When we have a solid foundation of masculine expression in our lives, the feminine feels safe and can finally relax. We settle into ourselves, trusting our inner knowing to guide us. We can be more in the moment, relaxing, enjoying, and taking in the beauty around us. When women have matured in this balanced way of living, when we have created a structure that provides enough of a sense of safety for us to relax and flourish, then the light we live becomes a beacon for others.

But given millenia of hyper-masculine behavior where

masculine energy has been twisted to protect the egos of people who hide their own weakness or fear, it often wreaks havoc. I might call that behavior *imbalanced yang energy* if we all knew Eastern wisdom. This toxic masculine expression often reverts to violence, using its strength and power to get its way, stratifying all options into the simplified opposites of right and wrong, with very little opportunity for negotiation or a middle ground.

Without the balancing feminine's trust in the strength of interpersonal connection to ensure positive outcomes, this insecure hyper-masculine ethos abuses its power, co-opting our societies, our political systems, our religions, and our financial institutions. It so dominates our everyday lives that we see it as "just normal."

No gender is immune to hyper-masculine behavior. It might be expressed outwardly towards others or inwardly upon oneself. When an internal sense of agency or control is lacking, it can often be observed in victim/abuser partnership dynamics. You likely recognize it in political figures, in those in positions of authority, at work, in intimate relationships, and in yourself, if you're honest.

It's much easier to see these behaviors in others than acknowledge them in ourselves. During the 2016 political season in the US, it didn't seem possible to me that a candidate who openly suggested grabbing women's genitals for the fun of it could possibly be elected. But when he was, I realized with horror the extent to which our culture still regards toxic masculine, power-over-ing behavior to be admired and lauded.

Hyper-masculine behavior is easy to see out there, in someone else! It uses power to dominate, shame, and bully.

We are disgusted by the way it silences dissent, punishes any weakness, and instills fear by abusing its power.

Yet what we despise in others, we often inflict upon ourselves, unconscious of how often and mercilessly we practice these very behaviors day to day.

Many of us learned to twist our healthy masculine energy of willpower and determination into forms of internal domination and suppression. So we use our strength of will to override our bodies' signals, pushing ourselves beyond what is healthy. We set over-enthusiastic goals and strong-arm our bodies to submit to our mind's timeline or goal.

We silence our body's pleas for rest or water or even to pee. We use well-acknowledged bullying behaviors to motivate ourselves to finish a project. We shame ourselves for making mistakes. We shut down our emotions to keep the peace. We rush and over-schedule, amping up cortisol and abusing our bodies and souls. And all the while, no matter how much we do or how well we do it, we feel like we're never doing enough, since doing is what is valued in an over-masculinized culture.

I know this all too well because these are habits I recognize in myself. I'd learned my early lessons well. My behavior was not that different from what Mr. Trump glorified. During those years of his presidency, I could see it all too clearly in myself.

We live in this hyper-masculine energy, still, regardless of the monumental steps toward gender equality of the last 75 years. Its damage is harming the Earth and every being that lives here. But like fish swimming in the tainted water of thousands of years of patriarchy, we hardly notice, to quote

Hafiz, the cruel knife we so often use on our own tender flesh and those of others.

It's time to speak up in defense of those values of the masculine that we most want to lead the way. But we can only change our world when we illuminate the shadow that hides within us. This is why I've spent the last fifteen years counseling and writing, working for the revival and awakening of the healing influence of healthy feminine energy for our world. It's this balance we must have if we are to survive as a species and be the light for the world.

How is feminine energy expressed? You know it when you feel it. And again, I'm not speaking about a particular gender! *Yin energy*, the Eastern term, feels warm and welcoming. It values connection over perfection, and is fluid and adaptable, flowing with ease within whatever circumstances it finds itself. Feminine energy trusts intuitive knowing and can find comfort and reassurance when no path is certain.

Our feminine essence is all-embracing, caring for those in need. It trusts a deeper connection to mystery beyond only analytic measurement and reason. Where healthy aspects of the masculine can be a solo actor, establishing safety by controlling the outer world through careful thought, planning, and action, feminine energy values emotion and the body's messages, relying on collaborative connection with others and the Earth, patiently cultivated over time.

Feminine energy loves spontaneity and delights in surprises. Its astute sensitivity carefully tunes into others' needs and responds with concern and compassion instead of reacting out of fear or threat. It finds beauty everywhere in the natural world. It finds joy in creative expression and loves to play.

Feminine energy brings the fun, the lightness and levity to life. It doesn't demand a win, but rather finds the possible wins in whatever situation or circumstance transpires.

No different than masculine energy, when the feminine feels unsafe, unsupported, or exhausted, a less healthy side tends to emerge. Then the feminine is likely to collapse and fall into victim thinking or behavior. She's too exhausted or despairing to make wise choices for healthy pleasure and is likely to numb out with substances and choices that help her avoid feeling the pain.

The feminine needs to feel safe and contained to flow in the innate love and connection that is its essence. And that connection is precisely what the masculine most longs for to express its most healthy protective and purposeful energies. A perfect marriage!

People lose their capacity to stay open and trusting when they don't feel safe. And when we need to be right we lose the chance for healthy joy.

When either energy is left in need of what's most primary for its health, we see a world like our own, unraveled by alienation and despair. And humans lacking in the joy I believe we were each meant to share.

Sadly in cultures where the feminine is denigrated in favor of traditionally masculine mores, where hyper-masculine domination wins, women learn to devalue their connection to their senses and the pleasure naturally found in the body. When sexual expression is twisted away from a healthy intimate balance that values connection and shared pleasure, women begin to distrust their body's messages.

Without **a respect for the natural connection that the feminine brings, erotic pleasure can be turned into a shallow perversion many women come to disdain.** So we learn to ignore our senses, devalue our emotions, and mistrust our pleasures. We work hard *doing* life, instead of living the feminine-infused life we most long for.

As a women's intimacy coach, it would be so easy to take sides here, to make it all about how f*cked up men are. But gender stereotyping doesn't demand much intelligence. And men suffer in less obvious but perhaps even more damaging ways in patriarchy.

As we explore how our less-than-healthy masculine *and* feminine energies have been running the show, we can direct our corrective focus toward what is healthy and healing for ourselves as well as society.

I'm seeing in my clients' lives—and my own—the powerful shifts that are possible with the dawning awareness of how to balance masculine and feminine energy.

No matter your gender, your healthy *yang* energy wants expression—it's what can hold and free the flow and joy of your *yin* feminine. As women cultivate the steady strength of our masculine oak-tree consciousness and structure so our feminine more fluid flow can improvise and play, we are able to create the more balanced and delight-filled life we were made for.

Peeling away what distorts our masculine essence may be the most important work of our time if we are to preserve the health of life on this precious Earth and become the beacons we were destined to be.

Then the extremes of unhealthy masculine pseudo-power and feminine indecision can relax toward our natural purposefulness and connection...and the joy that results.

Joy has a chance to catch us when we're awake to our senses and surroundings. That can only happen for me when I'm intending to be present here, in the moment, and not lost in my thoughts. A hawk landing on my fencepost. Spring announced by the first peepers' love calls from the wetland behind my house. Japanese maple leaves blazing red on a gray autumn day.

Without the masculine intention I fall victim to random and all too infrequent surprises that please me. Without the feminine delight in this moment's beauty and connection, I'll keep my nose to the grindstone until I'm too tired to do much more. Exhausted, I fall into a hyper-feminine stupor of apathy and indulgence.

Opportunities for joy come in a thousand variations, mostly small and easily missed. But receiving more of the multiple joys that await our attention demands my healthy masculine intention and action. I must be willing to be distracted from my agenda to catch the moment's offering, to tune into my senses enough to even notice what's there to delight me. This healthy balance allows the space for joy.

Joy likes to surprise me. It's not something I can plan. But it is my choice to receive it, which is made easier by conscious awareness.

Joy reminds me us that we've been gifted a life on a miraculously exquisite planet, here for our delight and badly in need of our protection.

When we empower our intention to create space to notice all that's here to delight us AND receive the moment-to-moment joy we were designed to experience, our light can't help but grow with us. Then we shine as beacons, illuminating the beauty of our own lives and creating a safe harbor for those looking to experience their own light.

About Mary

Mary Campbell is a long-time woman's empowerment and intimacy coach, ordained interspiritual minister, counselor, wedding officiant, and educator. She welcomes the cautious, the curious, and the bold to come alive at the intersection of the sacred and the senses. She is the author of the forthcoming book *The Pleasure Playbook: 13 Invitations for Awakening Joy*. Mary works privately with individuals and couples wishing to deepen their heart and body connection and balance their energies for more power, pleasure and play. She offers workshops and retreats for women and couples near her home in the Berkshire hills of Western Massachusetts, at Haramara Retreat Center in Mexico, and around the world. You can find her periodic blogs and offerings at DiviningBeauty.com, on FB at DiviningBeauty, videos on her YouTube channel, and on Instagram.

www.diviningbeauty.com

Chapter 2

The Spark Within

Velanda Samuel, MSW, LCSW

As I walked across the stage to receive my master's degree, I gazed out into the audience and observed my mother's smile and tears of joy as she witnessed her baby girl obtain a piece of paper which signified success, overcoming obstacles, and confirmation of faith. As I turned back to the stage to continue to walk to receive my degree, the song "Amazing Grace" so eloquently raced through my mind. With each step I sang to myself as the tears rolled down my face.

"Amazing grace! How sweet the sound that saved a wretch like me. I once was lost, but now am found, Was blind, but now I see."

Growing up I did not have role models in my immediate family who had attended college and could therefore encourage and inspire me to do the same. I would hear about college on television but never thought that it could or would be an obtainable goal of mine. My parents did not finish high school and out of my six siblings, my youngest brother and I were the only ones in our immediate family to complete high school. I enjoyed attending school as I was a smart kid who was able to problem-solve and I liked receiving validation for learning. However, my spark for learning disappeared when I was displaced from my school to attend a new school outside of the city.

Prior to being displaced I took delight in attending elementary school with my siblings in the neighborhood in which we were raised. My siblings and I would walk to school together. I had developed friendships at school that I looked forward to maintaining. One day while attending school in the 2nd grade I was informed by the teacher that I had been selected to participate in a program that would include me going to another school. She told me that it would be my last day attending Waverly Elementary school. While I really did not understand the magnitude of the change at the time, I was shocked. I could not believe this was happening. All I knew was that I felt safe attending school with my siblings and that I enjoyed attending school. I did well in school and I had friends I liked. When I got home from school, my mother confirmed what the teacher had told me. I had been chosen to attend a special program called Project Concern and that I would be taking a bus to a school called Hope Well in Glastonbury the next day.

Project Concern was initiated in 1966 as a busing program for underprivileged elementary school children who resided in the city of Hartford, Connecticut. The program's intent was two-fold: 1) to promote racial diversity in the suburban school setting and 2) to provide Hartford students with a high quality education that was otherwise not afforded by Hartford public schools. I learned later that there were thousands of suburban parents who crowded town hall meetings and demonstrated outside of the school to argue against accepting Blacks and Puerto Ricans from Hartford in the schools.

While attending school in Glastonbury I was able to make friends overtime, however, I also experienced harshness from some students who constantly called me derogatory names which made me feel unworthy. Attending a school outside of my environment also resulted in backlash from some family and friends who would ridicule me with names such as "white girl" and make fun of the way that I talked. As a result, I held back on showing my true intelligence. I was angry and had a need to be accepted which contributed to me conforming in many ways to fit in. During my middle school years I resisted learning and listening to teachers at school and I engaged in risky behaviors to fit in to avoid being further ostracized in my neighborhood.

I do not know the success rate of the students who attended the school from Hartford to Glastonbury through Project Concern but what I do know is that for me it was like two different worlds. It was difficult for me to fit in either, which caused me constant eternal agony. I yearned to be with my friends and family in the inner city although it was not a healthy environment.

Growing up my family moved often and my living environment consisted of living in a two bedroom apartment which resulted in some overcrowding as my siblings and I shared a bed together or some of us would sleep with my mother as she had a full size bed. It wasn't an odd living arrangement as it felt cozy and comfortable to be close to my family. It was fun and it was our normal. The environments where we lived included some form of working class people and also drug addicts, as well as violence and abuse which I witnessed almost daily outside of the home.

The violence and other abnormal behaviors that I witnessed outside of the home mimicked what I saw in my home growing up with my parents. My father was an alcoholic who was physically abusive to my mother. My mother was a passive woman. At times my mother would flee the home with us, and we would stay at my grandparents home only to return home after a couple of days when my father would sweet talk my mother into returning.

The saving grace for my mother and siblings and I was church. We would attend church four or five times per week. We received support, fellowship, and teachings of scripture there. My siblings and I sang in the choir which brought great joy to me, since as the baby girl of the family I really did not have a voice as my sisters cared for me and told me what to do. In the choir it was the same until I discovered that I could use my voice to go from the background of the choir to leading songs. Church was our place to be ourselves and to learn that there is a greater power that if you believed could give you strength to get through hard times.

When my mother was finally successful at freeing herself from the abusive hold of my father she became a single parent who had to work to care for seven children. While my mother went to work my younger brother and I were cared for by my older siblings who were in the midst of branching out on their own. This resulted in us being unsupervised and exposed to many inappropriate situations which included drinking, smoking and abuse by their boyfriends. This eventually showed up in my life as a teenager, too.

As a young teenager I started dating someone who was controlling and abusive. To me it wasn't odd behavior as it was a scene I had already watched growing up many times before. Now I was in the movie and was comfortable being in the bad scenes that almost cost me my life. I moved in with the person which was not approved by my mother and at that time. My father had moved back to his hometown of Florida. I was rebellious and adamant about being in a relationship that was similar to what I had already witnessed growing up. In a short amount of time I went from writing poetry, jumping rope, and playing double dutch with friends to being a live-in girlfriend with little to no support. Shortly after being in the relationship, I became pregnant.

As the result of becoming pregnant I left the Project Concern school as I entered 9th grade and enrolled in a school for pregnant teenagers called "Tap" which stood for Teenage Parent program. It was a school designed for students who were pregnant. The school offered regular academic classes, child growth and development, nutrition and parenting skills. It was a life saver for me as I had a desire to complete my education despite my pregnancy.

I always had a drive to accomplish goals however I lacked the role models to help me think bigger and beyond my circumstances. This slowed down the process of me finding my purpose. Although I attended school to obtain my high school diploma, I was not aware that I was actually able to go beyond the level of diplomacy and obtain a college degree. Here I was a young teenage mother who was in an abusive relationship with limited support and what appeared to be no way out. When I attempted to leave the relationship, I was emotionally and physically overpowered and afraid to call for help. It was like literally reliving my childhood story with everyone around me wearing blinders and along with me being comfortable with the scarcity of their life. My mother was busy working to make ends meet, my grandparents were getting older and my siblings who were all older than me with the exception of my baby brother were caught up in their own dysfunctional relationships. I felt alone and discouraged in many ways. The light of my life was my son who I loved dearly and who I was determined to offer a different life.

It was during that time that I learned that whatever I needed or wanted to achieve it had to come from God and from the strength that I had within me. Although I did not know how I was going to escape the hell that I was in, I had a burning desire to live and to grow. I began to pray daily and to think about the future that I wanted to have. I pictured myself living free, being independent, living in a peaceful home, and being happy. I also thought about my son who clearly possessed traits of intelligence as I had at an early age. I wanted to nourish and strengthen these traits. I started doing research on resources for people involved in relationships with domestic violence. I began to seek support. I prayed for a miracle to happen, and it did. One night while in another fighting match I prayed out loud during the moment of agony for God to take it away and to free me from the bondage. Just as the words finished leaving my mouth, he walked out of my life for good.

After completing school I enrolled in a program called Church Academy which was a job training and job placement program for inner city residents. There I learned many employability and soft skills that were required to enter the workforce.

Once I was hired to work at an insurance company, I began to explore the environment outside of the confined parameters in which I was conditioned to live. This led me to sign up for some college courses. Although I started off majoring in business administration, I had a burning desire to work in the field of social services. Without any experience in the social service field other than my own life experiences, I applied for a position at the Village for Families and Children and was hired as a full time program coordinator. As a program coordinator I managed afterschool programs at two inner city schools. It was so rewarding because as a child I had attended afterschool programs and remembered the joy that I experienced having a safe place to go to have fun. For me it was a full circle to now offer to children what brought me pleasure when I was young. As a result of finding my niche and working with children, I changed my college major and obtained an associate degree in Early Childhood Education. I continued my educational journey and enrolled in college at Saint Joseph University where I obtained a bachelor's degree in Child Studies. Although I enjoyed working with children as a program coordinator another opportunity presented itself to me as I was completing my internship working with teenage parents as an Employability Skills Coordinator. It was like déjà vu as I was now teaching others to gain employment skills which included me placing them at jobs to obtain hands-on skills.

The momentum of confidence and determination was in full throttle and I kept moving through the fear as I held on to courage and strength and my belief in my higher power to sustain and become my true self which was a smart, intelligent, eager and determined woman of dignity and grace. I pursued obtaining a master's degree in social work and shortly after obtaining my master's degree I was hired as a full time social worker for the Department of Children and Families. In pursuit of continued growth I set out to obtain clinical hours and direct supervision to become a therapist. As a therapist and owner of Breakthrough to Wellness Clinical Services, LLC, I help others find purpose through self-discovery and pain and to get rid of the limited beliefs that bind them to stay stuck in the pain. I help others find their strength within, just as I had to work on releasing the negative beliefs that I had thought about myself. I was able to break through the chains of distorted thoughts to reveal my strength and greatness.

As I walked across the stage to receive my master's degree, seeing the happiness on my mother's, husband's, and children's faces let me know that I was not alone and that I am worthy of self-love and greatness. I once was lost and now I am found. I was blind but now I see.

About Velanda

Velanda Samuel, MSW, LCSW and founder and CEO of Breakthrough Clinical Services, LLC. In her practice she goes by the title of Brain Health Strategist as she helps people who are trapped in negative limiting beliefs and thoughts to be free and find their strength within to reveal their authentic selves.

Velanda works with teenagers 16 years and older, adults, the elderly and the disabled, in the areas of anxiety, depression, post-traumatic stress disorder, grief and loss, as well as other life issues. Velanda has over 25 years of experience working with individuals and families in various capacities. Since the start of Breakthrough Clinical Services, LLC in 2015, she has grown her unique style of working in the field of mental health into a suite of programs.

Velanda has been featured as a frequent expert keynote speaker of mental health on various radio stations and on the news. Velanda is currently a radio personality at Powermuzic Radio as Breakthrough Vibrations with Velanda. Velanda is also a speaker and panelist at various conferences and retreats.

Velanda provides *Breakthrough to Wellness* workshops and group work on Self-Care and Holistic Wellness and she mentors master level clinicians on ways to obtain their licensure.

www.velandabreakthrough.com

Chapter 3

This Little Light of Mine

Kristi Borst, PhD

As soon as I sat down for my psychic reading, George said "You know you're a great healer, right?" I shrugged my shoulders. "You know you're a great healer, RIGHT?" he repeated. Again, I was non-committal.

I was at this spiritual fair as a vendor, sharing the energy, colors and delights of my energy-in-form fractal artwork. My art was a fairly recent creative endeavor, birthed in a meditative space of love-filled unity consciousness and utilizing my graphic design skills from a then 25-plus-year career. I was also providing hands-on blessings at my booth space, having been certified in Reiki and as a blessing-giver the prior year. Throughout the day, several friends had stopped by and urged me to get a reading with George L. I resisted their repeated prodding until there was a lull in the flow of visitors.

"You KNOW you're a great healer, right?" George repeated. This wasn't the first time I'd heard this... in each of the handful of prior readings I'd sat for, I'd been told I was a "great healer." I always blew it off, assuming each psychic intuitive could "see" my self-healings.

In the past year I had quickly healed a saw-blade cut to my index finger that could have used stitches. I pushed the skin together and bound the wound with a band-aid. The next morning, it was pretty well-sealed. On another

41

occasion, I had touched a hot oven rack with my forearm. Since I had read about multiple timelines I had intended to go to the timeline in which I didn't hurt myself. There was just a pale pink line instead of a serious burn the next morning. I had also eliminated symptoms of Reynaud's Disease I had been experiencing in my hands.

George repeated his seven-word query. Each time he pressed, I hemmed and hawed. He pressed on. My initial response of shrugged shoulders, morphed in my growing discomfort and frustration to "I guess so's." George pressed me further!

"You know you're a great healer, RIGHT?" he repeated for about the ninth time.

Finally, exasperated, I responded, "Well if I am, I don't know how to get THERE from here."

George chuckled softly and said, "that's because you performed a healing miracle as a very small child and scared the crap out of your parents. They told you to never do it again."

As he spoke these words, my mind pulled up a memory from more than 50 years prior... and it played out in my mind's eye.

My older brother and I, both preschoolers, were playing hide and seek. I made a giggle-filled getaway into the "log" fort our dad had built us. As I ran through the doorway of the fort, I scraped my face on one of the hewn logs and opened my cheek. My dad ran over and freaked out, seeing my face.

I was scared that he was angry with me, and I essentially closed the wound on the spot. I'm sure that shocked him even more—and he freaked out even more!

I know this sounds fantastic, and frankly, it is in every sense of that word! Had I not been amazed at the self-healing I had been achieving recently, I may have questioned it myself. Instead, in that instant and at age 55, it was as if I finally was handed the box and photo to the picture puzzle of my life! In addition, what had seemed like a random, even obscure, childhood memory fragment helped me OWN the healing memory more fully.

I stand in front of the rough hewn log that had cut me, gently tracing the jagged wood with one hand, my other hand caresses the same angle down my cheek.

I cannot tell you how many times this little memory fragment had played (seemingly randomly) in my adult life. It was short and lacked context, leaving me to wonder what it meant. Was this vague, random childhood memory my Soul's periodic knock-knock wake-up call?

Within this moment facilitated by George, I admired my younger, child-self. Somehow, despite her lack of life experience, she knew or was divinely guided to create a memory, anchored in a physical reference point. SHE was THE KEY to my RE-membering myself as Hope, Faith, Surrender, Grace... LOVE! I say "RE-membering" intentionally: RE (again), MEMBERing (bringing unto the SELF).

When my dad transitioned to spirit nearly 30 years ago, I found a little box of slides in his closet. One was a precious photo of me, taken around this time. A close-up camera captures my beaming dimpled face. My little belly boasts "Daddy's Little Angel," embroidered on overalls or a romper. I WAS a "good girl." I was also very obedient! I shut down this part of myself, hiding it so well that even I forgot it was there!

Here I sat with George. I had signed up for a 15-minute reading, so perhaps only a couple of minutes had elapsed; yet time seemed to stand still. So many thoughts, memories, and emotions flooded my mind. I had questions, but I also had clarity. I could understand my dad wanting to protect (or as George said "control") his toddler daughter. (Whatcha gonna do with a healing toddler, circa 1960, except hide the baby under a bushel basket?!?)

That was then, this was now! I was a "grown ass" woman searching for meaning in and to my life. I didn't need protecting. I wanted to be WHOLE! If I *was* a great healer, I knew it was time to OWN THAT! I said to George, "If I've made contracts with my dad or anyone else to shut any part of mySELF down, I want to rescind those contracts NOW!" George suggested we pray on that intention. We held hands very briefly and focused on that intention.

I went back to my art booth, amazed and so grateful. A woman for whom I had provided a hands-on blessing a short time earlier was waiting there for me. "I am not sure what you did when you touched me. You may have noticed I left you very quickly. I pretty much ran to the ladies' room. A flood of emotions rose from the depths of me, and I cried. I want to thank you so much for this, because I haven't been able to cry for years. It was such a healing experience for me." I don't remember what I said in response, but it warmed my heart to have been of service to her in this way! It also felt like a validation of George's message.

In the days and weeks after my reading, I was like a pig searching for truffles... rooting out the "boxes," "shoulds," rules, beLIEfs, etc... that I had "bought into" and otherwise allowed to confine or contain me. Using self-love, forgiveness, compassion, grace, I broke through each "wall" I found. I had been exploring the findings and theories of brilliant quantum physicists, and this helped me gain a deeper, less scientific understanding of our bodies and the way our world actually "works."

I embraced myself as a healer, inviting and re-integrating "my toddler self" to share her wonder, her wisdom and her Truths into my waking consciousness. She had been waiting, holding space for my return for more than 50 years. I was and AM so grateful!

We spend so much time looking outside ourselves, doing, attaining, certifying our skills, yet so much lies within our depths. Reuniting with this aspect of myself has brought a joy and wholeness to my present self that is hard to put into words. I REMEMBER who I AM.

I offered hands-on healing sessions, which were unique for each client. Frankly, I was putting my abilities "to the test." In each case, there was marked improvement in mind, body, spirit, and/or emotions. Sometimes there would be results that seemed miraculous. I could write volumes on this brief but amazing period, and will at some point.

I formally started Healing Resonance llc with Kristi Borst in 2013. My name is subordinate, recognizing that the work is coming through me, as me, but is Sourced by Universal Light/Love, Spirit, The Universe, Creator.

Later that year, I was invited to chat on a radio show. I described the quantum-level, multi-dimensional work I offer, that crosses time and space and facilitates marked mind-body-spirit-emotions shifts for my clients. "Similar to a computer reboot," I said. "It's like they get a Perspective

Reboot®" and the name of my spiritual energy healing and empowerment process was born!

In the nearly ten years since my homecoming to SELF, I've supported many adults and children, individually or in their union as couples and families, in their quest for/toward more and better. Whether they are feeling stuck, anxious, fearful, depressed, ill, diseased, lost, I am able to support their forward movement, sometimes taking them back to the state of RE-membering through my healing resonance. I guide and assist in releasing what no longer serves them and Our Highest Good.

The childhood healer within me thrives! Childhood healing and re-integration for inner peace is a large part of my practice because many times these long-ago woundings can be at the core of our pain and struggle. I am particularly adept at sleuthing out and illuminating self-limiting beLIEfs and other non-physical aspects of the self that are manifesting at the root of unease and/or disease.

While we're urged to take a pill when we have pain or illness symptoms, these are our bodies' way to communicate where we are off balance. Pain and illness are not random; we are not the victim. Some of the sickest people are actually the most powerful creators, they merely haven't understood their power, have mis-directed their focus, and have not been grounded in Love.

I help my clients understand and improve the "weakest link" within the body or immune system. As we resolve and release trauma, fear, or the fragmented self, they can more freely create abundant wellness and joy.

My work and ongoing journey toward self-actualization have allowed me to see beyond what meets the eye and the

MRI and to ponder "why can't I?" after all! As we live more mindfully, we are able to see(ze) opportunities previously hidden amid lies within our beLIEf systems. These illusions are unique to our experiences and "stories." Yet, they often lead/carry us further and further from Truth, our intended destination, dream, desires, purpose, etc...

In the most basic terms, LOVE connects us and helps our amazing bodies to heal; fear separates us and is like a monkey wrench in the body systems and in our world. We live in these bodies that tell us we are individual and separate, and we are urged to conform and blend and fit in. And yet, in Truth, we are here because we each hold a unique radiance of light and love. We recognize that spark easily in newborns and infants. It's time to re-ignite your spark!

Thirteenth century Persian philosopher and mystic Rumi shared "You are not a drop in the ocean. You are the entire ocean in a drop." I'm sure at some point, you've experienced our interconnectedness. You think of someone and they call or text, or you call someone and they say "I was just thinking about you." Our connectedness allows me to connect at a quantum level in a phone call with someone physically situated across the planet and, with their permission, affect their mind, their body, their emotions, their energy flow, their countenance.

Many people are seeking, even chasing, a grandiose yet elusive Life Purpose. However if your path is not clear it may not be ready OR you may be settling if you moved forward at this point. I'd like to suggest that your purpose is right here and is readily achievable.

"All you've gotta do is BE!" In each day, regardless of what life throws your way, respond with love. You may have to shift

47

your focus a bit, but in all challenge there is opportunity! Find gratitude, anticipation, hope, peace. Aim to make our world a better place by showing up as Love, compassion, generosity, forgiveness. Almost immediately your quality of life will improve. You'll reap the benefits of being happy, regardless of your job, status, or any other outward measure.

Am I a great healer? Absolutely! Yet, I wouldn't be here as healer, mother, and wife without my husband of now 40-plus years. When we met, Spirit said "he's the one." Joe accepted me as perfect, even when my light was fractured internally and I didn't remember how to turn on my beacon. He, in essence, healed the healer. So, perhaps that makes *him* the "Great Healer." In reality, we are all healing (or wounding) one another.

Like Dorothy who always had the power to return home from Oz, we have always been cherished, treasured, guided, protected, and loved. When we seek love outside of ourselves, we can come up empty-handed. Yet within lies a well-spring... it just may be buried beneath obsolete programming, fears, traumas, and fractured aspects of our True Self! It's a virtual treasure chest in there!

We have to know we are lost before we seek to find. This may be when we truly observe and question the path we're on. Perhaps, we've been missing directional signs in our rush forward. We may come to a halt in the midst of overall melancholy, feeling stuck, anxious, unhappy or gripped by physical pain and/or disease. Sleuth out your internal "hiding spots" and flood yourself with compassion, love, and light.

If you'd like support and guidance, please call on me. We can certainly be too close to "our stories" and even too deep within our hide and seek game to remember we're hiding.

Fortunately, we don't have to look too far! Often the answers we seek are hiding in plain sight.

As you step across the Earth on this journey, will you leave angry footprints or will you seed love? Intend to make that choice evermore consciously. Several years ago, I noticed that when I went out in public, people would smile at me. Then I realized that I was always walking around with a smile on *my* face. The way we express ourSELVES affects and attracts what we experience and receive! The time is ripe for RE-membering who you are and to SHINE, my friends! Be the Beacon.

You are not only enough, you are a treasure, here for a reason. You are not only loved, you ARE Love. Back in the day, I taught Sunday School and we sang the song... "This little light of mine, I'm gonna let it shine, let it shine, let it shine, let it shine!" Let that be your motto for a month, and see how your life shifts.

I'd like to leave you with this gentle nudge. That queasy feeling you sometimes feel in the pit of your stomach is not fear or anxiety; it is your greatness urging you forward.

Watch your beLIEfs and embrace the power in your unwritten story. Your future is truly unlimited. RE-member the myriad aspects of Self, let your light shine, and soar.

With Love, Kristi

About Kristi

Kristi Borst, PhD is an intuitive spiritual healer and founder of Perspective Reboot®, an energy-healing process for increased joy, wellness, self mastery, and ascension. She lives in southern Maine, splitting her time between a home nestled in the woods and a treetop "summer camp," offering big-sky and lake views. Kristi is blissfully married to her college sweetheart and is very proud of their two grown daughters.

Kristi Borst offers spiritual counseling and healing for all ages via private, couples, and group sessions, both in-person in southern Maine and worldwide, via phone or internet.

Kristi's Healing Resonance llc website offers an online calendar, so you may book 24/7. Kristi has built a catalog of pre-recorded, chakra-healing, breast wellness and inner peace sessions labeled "Kore Healing^{SM} with Kristi." You may also view and order her fractal energy-in-form art on her site. Kristi shares myriad support and upliftment via her free blogs, social media and her expansive Perspective Reboot® podcast.

www.HealingResonance4.Me

IG & FB @healingresonancellc

twitter #kristiborst

Chapter 4

When My Light Got Lit

Akanke Rasheed

It was 1989. I was 26 years old and had never even heard the word "seminar" before, let alone participated in one. But there I was curiously scanning all the interesting books on the vendor tables in the back of the room. The pleasant smell of lemongrass filled the room and soft music played with chanting sounds.

What had I entered into? Another universe? Me, a young black woman from the hood at an evening seminar with a bunch of white folks called "Create a Life You Love." I was waiting for the new friend who invited me to arrive. I had just met him the Sunday before while gazing at books inside the Truth and Treasures Bookstore at Hillside International Truth Center, where we both attended Sunday church service.

Hillside was known to be one of the most progressive churches in Atlanta and had become my home for spiritual cultivation. It was founded by Dr. Barbara King—a giant soul—literally and figuratively. At 6'5", her presence was powerful. She was a towering figure with a strong raspy voice, a warm infectious smile, and a deep love for God that steered her progressive mission at Hillside. She passionately infused new age principles into Christian theology, including metaphysical discussions about the mind, body, and soul and positive affirmations that were recited in unison by the congregation to help us manifest greater self-love, confidence, and abundance, individually and collectively. Powerful celebrity speakers like Iyanla Vanzant and Les Brown were regular guests. Hillside was a place where the African-American community found spiritual inspiration to thrive and where I found fuel for my personal growth and ascension.

As everyone waited for the event to begin, there was a lot of chatting, laughing, networking, and even some chanting. The vibe was positive and uplifting and I found myself smiling curiously the whole time. It felt right and wonderful and very different to be there. This wasn't ladies night or after hours with cocktails, this was another type of hook-up. I continued glancing over the wide range of books on subjects I never imagined existed and stopped to look inside the titles that intrigued me. I will never forget *Personal Power Through Awareness: A Guidebook for Sensitive People* because I had grown to be sensitive about my mother telling me I was "too sensitive." I noticed ones that were familiar to me because I had seen them in the church bookstore, *Think and Grow Rich*, *As a Man Thinketh*, and *The Law of Attraction*. I became mesmerized by the various books and excited that there were books like them that could help guide me to a deeper understanding of myself and life. My universe was expanding.

Louis arrived just as everyone was invited to take a seat, signaling the seminar was starting. I quickly paid for the books I wanted and we sat near the front. The featured presenter was introduced. Her name was Sondra Ray. She was tall and slender with vibrant red hair and a wide smile. She looked Scottish or Irish but spoke like a southerner. She was the author of *Loving Relationships*. There was a table at the front of the room dedicated to her book and other self-help merchandise.

She welcomed us with boisterous questions, "Are you ready to create a life you loooove!?!? Are you ready to experience greater love in your relationships?"

"Yes! Yes!" we all said.

By the end of the evening, the journey she had taken us on enlivened us by helping us imagine a life free from self-imposed limitations and filled with the willingness to forgive in order to experience more love, abundance, joy, and grace. I was starlit and teary-eyed. What unfolded within the two hours was a journey of deep reflection into our hopes and desires, our hurts, inhibitions, and past disappointments. We were asked to think deeply. What could life become if we uncovered the hidden beliefs that we didn't even know we had but nonetheless had been holding us back and keeping us from progressing? How could love emerge more organically and how could our life change if we could be truly forgiving—100%? What might it look and feel like to have relationships that enjoyed a soulful, heart-centered and spiritual intimacy and connection?

The room pulsated with a mixture of emotions as we all thought about creating a life we loved.

Well, I already *had* a life I loved. As a 26-year-old who had dropped out of college to work, I landed a wonderful job working for an accounting software company. To be an employee at a software company in 1989 is like working for Microsoft, Google, or Apple today. It was a big deal, and I was climbing the corporate ladder. I started as a mail clerk in the accounts payable department. Within a year I was promoted to the position of Accounts Payable Administrator processing invoice payments—paying the company's bills using the company's own proprietary accounting software system. As one of three AP Administrators, I became a wiz at understanding the software system. I learned it beyond just entering raw data—invoice numbers, amounts, and due dates—to generate check payments in the system. Over the course of a year, I learned the system inside and out, which positioned me as an ideal candidate to work in the Technical Support Division helping our clients troubleshoot using our accounts payable system. As such, when a technical support position opened up, I applied for it and I was accepted into a trainee position for 90 days as a prelude to being promoted into the position. I was excited! I was also envied by my peers.

The future was looking great for this college dropout from the hood. Being a technical support rep would give me a salary of $45K in 1989, working alongside middle-aged white men who had bachelors and masters degrees in technical fields like Computer Information Systems. I was already living a life I loved!

In addition to my promising corporate trajectory, I had my own luxurious apartment. I had a sporty two-seater black Mazda RX7, with a manual transmission. I loved shifting those gears! I eventually traded it in for a beautiful, metallic blue BMW 320i. I also enjoyed a decent social life and stayed out of trouble for the most part by having only a few close friends that I had known since high school. I was going to church regularly and studying metaphysical principles about mindset, spirituality, and manifesting dreams. I often thought about life and what it could be if I continued climbing the corporate ladder. Who could I become for myself and my family? If I kept climbing and succeeding I would eventually become a technical trainer, traveling to different client locations. It was an exciting future and my life was good!

At the end of that seminar, Louis and I were blown away and everyone was invited to continue exploring life more deeply. Sondra's network of trainers offered other events that took deeper dives into self-discovery. The next one was coming up soon—a weekend training called The LRT, an acronym for Loving Relationship Training. It was two and half days looking into matters of the heart and mind, removing blocks that prevented us from experiencing more love and freedom within ourselves that promised to impact our relationships positively and powerfully. I didn't think twice! My flame had been lit! I registered and paid in full right away, and couldn't wait for the weekend to arrive. I read Sondra's book and peeped inside the others I bought.

The weekend arrived quickly and the LRT Workshop was amazing and dynamic. It turned up the flame even more. I became more open to express myself, to get in touch with my inhibition, my passions, my fears, my desires, and *my* life more deeply. Who and what could I become if I had more faith in myself, in "The Universe," and in the promise of an unknown rich with possibilities?

Louis and I were the only African-Americans in the LRT workshop. I wondered why. I wished that more of my friends and family could experience what we were experiencing. However, I also felt it was too New Age for anyone else that I knew. Collectively, we had never learned about the concept of self-awareness, that thoughts were "things," and that there was a dynamic process at play in our lives in which we were co-creating our reality based on our thoughts, beliefs, and actions. We had never heard of the concept of conscious and subconscious thoughts. The LRT exposed me to a lot. It was life-changing. I felt blessed and my new quest became to become fully "self-actualized."

At the end of the weekend workshop, I was emotionally full and mentally exacerbated. We had gone through many iterations of unearthing deeply held ideas and beliefs. Self-reflection and self-examination take a lot of energy and necessarily stir up many emotions including joy, anger, sadness, and shame.

Sondra was a compassionate facilitator. She coached us and gave us tools like affirmations, conscious breathing, and writing to help cultivate self-love, self-compassion, and self-acceptance. We released painful experiences that had been negatively impacting us. We forgave people in our lives who we felt had wronged us, hurt us, or otherwise injured our hearts in some way or vice-versa. We were told we had to free ourselves from emotional blocks and mental clutter in order to be freer and create a life that was filled with more love and deeper trust and vulnerability.

I was excited about everything that happened in the weekend workshop. I started thinking about taking a day or two off from work to process and integrate things. A lot had shifted for me. Then, at the conclusion on the Sunday session we were invited to consider an even longer training program. *Wait, there's more?!?!* Hearing that other opportunities were available excited me, but I gasped when I heard it was a six months long program that would take place in Connecticut, and cost thousands of dollars. *Whew! No, I could not sign up for that!*

I went back to work. My energy and attitude was different, my light was brighter. At work, I had proven I could earn a higher technical position. I knew the job would be easy for me and I was doing very well as a trainee. Meanwhile, I also could not stop thinking about all that I had been exposed to through The LRT and the idea of enrolling in the upcoming program in Connecticut. I daydreamed about it. Louis was interested in taking the program too, but neither of us could see the way forward easily. I would have to completely unroot my life. I would have to request a leave of absence or quit and neither would be ideal for me as a new trainee. My corporate career was important to me. Could I let go of it? That did not seem like a prudent option, but that is exactly what I did!

I put my faith in the possibility of expanding my life beyond what I could imagine in that moment. I had to envision getting to know more about myself, my inner dimensions, and how to create a new life that I could love even more than what I already had. I was strategic. I didn't quit right away. I first borrowed $2000 from my 401K savings to make the down payment for the course. Then I gave my two weeks' notice. The remaining money from my plan would be processed after I terminated completely. I informed the leasing manager at my apartment complex that I had to relocate urgently. This presented issues with me having to break my lease. I had to make some difficult decisions and I remember feeling like the obstacles I faced were my tests. Louis and I started dating, he found money for his down payment and we planned our journey to Connecticut. Weeks later, on our way to Connecticut, he asked me to marry him. I said yes and we decided to take a trip to NYC and get married by a judge in the courthouse. He was a real estate developer and needed to go to NYC to meet a former business partner to get money that was owed to him.

He never got it and that was a part of our tests too.

My mother thought I had lost my mind. She witnessed me quit my job, move out of my apartment and leave Atlanta to enroll in a "program." Had I joined a cult? Even though I assured her it was not a cult, I remember struggling to explain to her exactly what it was I was embarking on. On some level, I didn't exactly know myself. I just knew it felt right. I enjoyed learning and discovering more about myself and life. She looked at me sideways with concern, but she never tried to stop me. She cautioned me to be very careful and she wanted all the names, phone numbers and addresses of where I was going to be, who I was staying with, and what I was involved with, and she definitely thought I was crazy for marrying Louis!

During the six-month program the cohort meet regularly, we studied *A Course in Miracles*, learned rebirthing, earthed our "personal lies"—the false beliefs that sabotaged our conscious desires. We also traveled internationally to Greece and Spain as part of our learning experience.

Enrolling in the program proved to be a major milestone in my life. It turned up the flame and fueled my personal journey of ascension exponentially, but not without some challenges, confrontations, and deep excavations of some old conditioning within me. The experience proved that personal growth was not all warm and fuzzy, but it opened me up, gave me greater awareness, and helped me begin the journey of a lifetime—and today has inspired me to create my own program called The Sacred Journey of Ascension™.

By the time we finished the program, I had learned and grown a lot. I had started and stopped smoking cigarettes and my BMW got repossessed. I had also decided to divorced

Louis, file bankruptcy, and move back in with my mother! It sounds like failure, but it was all good. I had to let go of certain things internally and externally in order to embrace new things. Everything that I learned changed me deeply.

At that first evening seminar in in 1989 I was Leslie Ann. Today, I am Akanke [Tiamoyo] Rasheed. My name change was another of several milestones to come that were symbolic outcomes of my new self and my new awareness. I wanted aname that connected me to my African ancestry—ancestry that I had been taught to hate. *Akanke* is a Yoruba word that means, "To know her is to love her." *Tiamoyo* is a Swahili name that means, "One who helps in beautiful things." *Rasheed* is an Arabic name that means "One who strives for spiritual development." My name represents a blend of my African culture and Muslim idenity as well as my personal aspirations of who I strive to be.

It's been a long time since I connected with the LRT trainers, Bob and Mallie Mandel, but I'm delighted that I recently reconnected with Bob for the first time since 1989. I asked him to recall why they created the six-month program. He replied,

"We created it to support people from around the world who were involved in the burgeoning personal growth movement. The idea was to provide long-term training and evolution instead of a one day or weekend seminar, which were quite popular in those days. So, you lived together in group houses, met frequently as one group every month, received private sessions, and also, we travelled all together, a few times to uproot ourselves from the familiar environment. The focus was on loving relationships, healing birth trauma and unconscious family patterns, self-esteem, and leadership."

For me the six-month program was a deep dive into

myself, shining the light on my "old conditioning," the good, the bad, the ugly in order to release, unlearn, and transform

From that program, I decided I wanted to help change others. I wanted to teach self-discovery within the African American community. I was excited about this possibility but was also annoyed, dismayed, disappointed, and sometimes angry. Why wasn't self-discovery and self-awareness already being taught in my community? Why was I the only African American in those trainings? Why had I not been taught about the importance of my self-awareness, how to cultivate an empowered mindset, and encouraged to think deeply, not follow the herd, and become a beacon? Why was there no class, bootcamp, seminar, or course in my community that taught this stuff and helped cultivate self-empowerment and personal growth? Surely, God has intended this for everyone! Why in God's beautiful names wasn't this being blasted everywhere—at school, at home, at church, on TV? Why weren't more people who looked like me benefiting from these teachings and concepts already?

I now accept that sometimes the best way to answer a question is by creating a solution to the problem it confronts. Today, I realize I was blessed to participate in ways that others couldn't or didn't know about because I was chosen to be a beacon. It is part of God's divine order that I've had so many opportunities to travel, learn, and enroll again and again in courses that have benefitted me. I feel blessed and honored that since 1989, I've continued learning, growing and helping others do the same.

Just as the bee that travels from flower to flower getting the sweet nectar, it has been part of my divine assignment to journey away from my hometown in order to live around the world, enroll in different programs, earn various certifications, attend lots of courses and retreats, and learn from great mentors and teachers that I can give the sweetness of what I've learned to integrate and embody to others. My deep dive into personal-development and self-actualization for all these years has been part of my divine assignment so that I can be a light for others by teaching what I've learned. Assignment accepted with joy!

About Akanke

Akanke Rasheed is a woman whose greatest passions are spirituality and personal growth. In 1989, at the age of 26, she was faced with the decision to stay comfortable in her fast-growing corporate career at a leading software company which she really enjoyed or take the risk and quit her job in order to enroll in a six-month deep dive personal development program in Washington Depot, Connecticut. Those six months turned into a lifetime as she pursued her path of ascension and self-actualization, with its many twists and turns, joys and many challenges, lessons and blessings.

Akanke is on the path of a spiritual warrior—always looking for the spiritual lessons in life. She lives with inspiration fueled by her love for Source, which makes her a compassionate leader and an effective coach and mentor. She considers it an honor, blessing, and unique responsibility to help uplift others and she does so with a deep sense of love, grace, gratitude, and authenticity. She is a certified transformation retreat leader who also has certifications in life coaching, nutrition coaching, spiritual intelligence assessments, and personality profiles assessments. Additionally, she has a bachelor's degree in film and television and has produced and hosted TV and radio talk shows and short documentaries.

www.akankerasheed.com

Chapter 5

Confidence & Beauty

Mary Carangelo, MSW

To me, there are three levels of dress: 1) Embracing Your Ugly, 2) Gym Days, and 3) Your Best Version.

When I refer to embracing "Your Ugly," I am not calling you ugly or the way you dress ugly. I am referring to the days when we hold on to that feeling of just waking up—the unkept, unbrushed, first-thing-in-the-morning look. The weather may be lousy or you are feeling lousy, and your form of dress is sweats, wrapped in your favorite comfy blanket. You are trying to hold onto that cocoon of warmth and comfort you had in bed. Your agenda consists of streaming Netflix and your daily washing ritual may or may not occur. Yes, you're entitled to a few of these "super relaxed" days!

The second level of dress is when you pull on your workout clothes to begin your day with morning exercise. Time and tasks propel your day forward, lunch time comes and goes and working out becomes a fleeting thought. Now it's dinner time and your tasks are done except for the one task that motivated your choice of dress this morning. You now change out of your workout clothes and back into your pajamas. Your intention was good but the follow through just wasn't there.

The third level of dress is when you want to present the best version of yourself. You choose outfits to show you are confident, a beacon to others, a leader, a woman in charge.

Your clothing is communicating to everyone who you are. What are you saying?

Choosing what to wear each day is typically the first decision that you make. Do you start your day staring into your closet feeling frustrated because you have absolutely NOTHING to wear!? This is quite a paradox as I am positive that most of the clothes in your closet ended up being there because YOU bought and put them there. Now the big question: Why would you purchase or KEEP clothes that do not fit your current size, body shape, or lifestyle?

The answer to this question is simple.

You are living in the "remember when" world; when you were skinnier, when you were younger, when you had a different lifestyle. You are living in the past. Your closet was NOT meant to be the scrapbook of your life.

If I were to open the door to your closet this very minute, what would it tell me about you? (No, you do not have time to go and straighten it up!) Do you have old college sweatshirts? Concert T-shirts? Clothes with tags on them? Clothes that no longer fit you?

Of course, you do! We all do! It's hard to let go.

Getting dressed with intent is no easy task! It takes knowledge, an understanding of design and a willingness to embrace the proportions of your body. It takes a lot of courage to REALLY look at yourself and see the beauty reflected. Loving that image and knowing what style and colors suit you are the first steps in helping you to purchase with purpose. Curating a wardrobe that serves you encourages self-love and a communication style that is in alignment with who you are TODAY!

I think of closets as a sacred space that should be functional and provide you with choices of dress that give you comfort, confidence, and the ability to communicate to the world your intent. Clothes carry memories and are imprinted with the energy or feeling from the last time you wore them.

The simple, beautifully tailored black dress I wore to my mother's funeral made me melancholy every time I saw it. I have chosen to remove this dress from my closet as it is not a memory I want to revisit at the beginning of each day. I have also removed pants that no longer fit my current body shape and size. Every time I put on a pair of pants that didn't fit, my frustration rose and my negative self-talk began to whisper in my ear. It was so liberating to purge my closet and keep only things that fit and that I liked. Now it takes me two minutes to get dressed AND I feel fantastic when I walk out the door!

Comfort and design are a few of the key factors I look for when purchasing clothing. If it is too tight, uncomfortable, itchy, or pulls, I will not buy it. I purchase with a purpose and spend my money on items that make me look great and feel good! I believe this stems from my personal style story and my childhood experiences growing up around textiles.

My mother worked second shift at a textile mill and one of the benefits was being able to bring home material that had slight imperfections. Reams of corduroy, velvet, and cotton were piled high in the back room of our duplex house. They provided a great resource for my grandmother, a fabulous seamstress who spent hours pressing on the pedal of her old black cast iron sewing machine stitching together patterns. Not only was my grandmother a fabulous seamstress but she was also visually impaired. Even with one glass eye, she was able to magically produce outfits that had her creative flair.

When I was around 8-years-old, my grandmother designed a stunningly beautiful ensemble that is emblazoned in my memory forever. It was a blue velvet cape with matching blue velvet shorts; not just any blue but the color of the sky. The reason I remember this outfit so vividly was NOT the way I looked in it, but the way I FELT.

Easter Sunday was a day to wear your finest outfits, and my mother dressed me in my new velvet cape with matching shorts. As I filed in with the other parishioners, I noticed a heaviness to my outfit. With all the activity of kneeling, standing, and sitting, I started to feel slightly uncomfortable. But when I left for communion the problem became clear. That heaviness and feeling of being uncomfortable was the friction, sticking, and resistance of the velvet rubbing against itself. My grandmother had used a thickly threaded velvet meant for upholstery to sew my Easter outfit. Every step was like having velcro patches attached to the interior of my thighs. The material stuck and bunched with every step. I felt the most uncomfortable I have ever been in any outfit. I am sure you will not be surprised to find that I currently do not own any clothing made from velvet.

If I asked you to remember a time when you felt the most uncomfortable, I wonder what your story would be?

Conversely, if I were to ask you a time in your life when you felt the most beautiful, comfortable and confident; I wonder what you were wearing at the time? In asking this particular question to multiple women, I assumed that many of them would say the day they were married or when they were going to a special event. I was very surprised and delighted to find that this memory was anchored by many different experiences.

One woman, Heather, 11-years-old, was standing on a rock in the middle of a field wearing the most colorful T-shirt. It was a multi-colored top of burnt orange, black and yellow. These colors were prominently displayed on the flowy material that was sewn under the arms. As Heather reached for the sky, the most magnificent butterfly wings appeared! She twirled on that rock, feeling beautiful, confident, as if she could do anything and fly over any obstacle.

Another woman had just finished a triathlon, her face was sweaty and red. She was hot and felt like a fish out of water in the neoprene wetsuit that helped her to stay afloat in the mile swim. She had conquered her fears, reached her goals, and her inner strength was reflected as a feeling of beauty and confidence. She stood just a little taller and her eyes reflected the love and admiration she had for herself and for a job well done!

My final example takes place in Paris. Patricia had accompanied her husband on a business trip, and for a special evening out, he took her to the restaurant at the top of the Eiffel Tower. A romantic dinner for two in the city of love. She chose to wear a simple black dress with delicate pearls. As her husband sat across from her, she saw the love and admiration in her husband's eyes and felt like the most beautiful woman in the world.

The idea that your choice of dress can make you feel a certain way is becoming quite clear, but did you know that it can also make you smarter?

In a study coined *Enclothed Cognition,* college students were randomly assigned to wear a white lab coat that they believed was a doctor's coat. They were then asked to identify the color of the letters that spelled different color words. If the word red was printed in blue lettering, students would need to respond blue. Those who wore the "doctor's coat" scored 50% higher than those who did not.

How you dress can impact the way you feel about yourself and the way that others perceive you. A doctor's coat is identified with intelligence and authority. With this premise, it is not surprising that the "doctor's coat" helped students to tap into their intelligence. They were already intelligent, but their level of confidence in their ability to respond correctly improved based upon how they felt in their clothing. A nobel prize winner, Isaac Bashevis Singer, said, "What a strange power there is in clothing!" I believe that how you dress is a powerful tool and when used with purpose, truly impacts your level of confidence and how you communicate with those around you.

Is your outfit choice helping or hindering your self-confidence? What can you do to improve the success of selecting outfits to help you showcase the best version of yourself?

Purposely purging your closet and discarding clothes from the "remember when" era is one way you can begin to curate a wardrobe with function and intention. It will allow you to curate a wardrobe that is in alignment with your life and who you are!

How do you purge your closet?

- Take absolutely everything out.

- Get ready to try on every piece.

- Look at yourself in a full length mirror (front and back).

- Make 3 piles: 1) to discard, 2) to keep, 3) to donate.

- Place back into your closet only the clothes that fit your body and your life.

Does this take time? YES!!! But I promise that you will feel so much better after this process. Ultimately, you will save time and be less stressed when getting dressed each day.

Whatever your style or choice of dress, YOU need to own it. When you think of Diane Keaton or Whoopi Goldberg, they continually express their individuality by the way they dress. Can you imagine Whoopi in a tailored Ralph Lauren dress or Diane Keaton in a Jessica Parker dress? It would be like taking a square peg and trying to bang it into a round hole. No matter how hard you tried, it just wouldn't fit.

I bet you have friends that dress a certain way...you can't explain it...but it's just THEM! I have a friend who LOVES to mix formal wear with combat boots. It looks amazing on her because it works with her energy, her personality, and her sense of fun! If I wore that, I would just look plain silly!

Your clothing choices carry memories, imprint feelings, and the light from within shines a little brighter. These choices are a major contributor to your sense of self. Loving who you see in the mirror each day is the first step in setting intent for all the great things you are going to accomplish!

So beautiful lady, take risks in your dressing, explore styles outside your comfort zone, and don't stop until your light shines brighter. Your closet is your sacred space, a place of self-expression. Have fun with it, and know that the greatest love you can ever receive is from yourself. Be your own beacon, leading yourself with confidence and beauty will follow.

About Mary

Mary Carangelo is a stylist, fashion therapist and an entrepreneur. She has been styling women for the past 12 years, helping them to "up-level" their look by "up-loving" themselves. Building confidence by teaching clients to purchase with a purpose, in alignment with who you are today.

Mary has her BSED and MSW in Family Therapy. Once married with children, she was fortunate to be able to stay at home. Her love of connecting women and passion for entrepreneurship, led her to the world of fashion. Instead of doing Family Therapy, she transitioned to Fashion Therapy, helping women to identify their own style story.

www.MCstyling.com

www.marycarangelo.cabionline.com

Email at: Fashiontherapistxo@gmail.com

Chapter 6

Go All In

Barb Pritchard

I believe everything happens for a reason. 2020 was eye-opening for so many of us for a plethora of reasons. For me, it was a line of demarcation between being the captain of the struggle bus and joyfully hopping off to take the keys to abundance within my business. It was when I decided to go all in, embrace my authenticity, and take the first step in my woo-woo walk.

I've been designing for over 20 years now. I worked in corporate for many of those years and learned loads of strategy, skills, and secrets that consistently and successfully move the needle for Fortune 100/500 clients. But, like many of us who cut our teeth on corporate culture, I felt unfulfilled and dreamed of becoming my own boss.

Very early on I began moonlighting on the side, applying the principles I learned in college and at corporate toward helping small businesses with a purpose. It scratched that itch to help others. It also provided that freedom I yearned for that I'd never have in my corporate career. I didn't have to cut through all the red tape to make things happen. No silly office politics. I'm not a brown-noser and despise stroking people's egos. I'm the type of gal who says what she means and means what she says. It's not in me to provide an empty compliment. Freelancing on the side felt good! I could make a difference in the lives of the businesses I helped and clients would come to me by way of referral. It felt freeing and easy.

When 2020 reared its ugly head, I found myself furloughed (eventually laid-off) and chomping at the bit to go full time in my business. I was ready to experience that ease full time!

But the sudden realization of getting clients became urgent, frantic even, as opposed to the casual approach I took when I was "gainfully" employed and running a side-biz. I felt like I was floundering, desperate, only making ends meet because I was receiving pandemic relief. I felt so lost and forever on the search for something that I couldn't quite put my finger on. I just wanted more! More clients! More... *something!* But those clients didn't come and my past clients were pulling tightly on their purse strings, understandably, to stay afloat. *Something* was missing!

I tried to do what the big names were saying led to their success: show up, niche down, do this, be that. I took course after course, feeling lost and confused because what was supposed to work, well, wasn't. I had the skills that paid the bills in my side business, but wow this was way different from what I expected! And I still felt that something was missing.

In 2020, there was talk of a new paradigm shift, an awakening of sorts. I had no idea what the heck that meant. All I knew was that the more news I read, I continually felt more and more disillusioned with societal norms. That's not unusual for me, I've always been a bit of a rebel and a cheerleader of the underdog. But with the happenings of 2020 being politicized with a sprinkle (or more) of religiosity on top, I was questioning everything again.

It took me back to being 16, when Ellen DeGeneres came

out and announced to the world she's a lesbian. I remember so many people loved her show, Ellen, but when she came out, many boycotted it for religious reasons. I couldn't get behind that. I took to questioning family and friends who were among that group to try and understand the why behind it. I questioned the Bible, the teachings, God, everything!

I've always been a curious gal. I was fortunate enough to have an understanding dad who indulged my curiosity. I'm sure I drove him nuts with all the "why" questions, but he never lost his patience with me, instead he saw it as an opportunity for me to learn. Dad was a rocket scientist, he understood the value of questioning and creating hypotheses. Interestingly enough, Dad, a patent-holding scientist, was also a Christian. And when the Ellen incident happened, I asked him many questions that he just couldn't answer beyond "because the bible says so." Because *anyone* says so wasn't a good enough explanation when I was 4, it certainly didn't cut it at 16. Nor does it at 40.

2020 had me asking many of those same questions, feeling the same, unsatisfied feelings at the same, lame answers I received. I couldn't wrap my head around how people were acting in the name of religion. I questioned everything again God, the Bible, the principals, and was left reeling with disappointment and still feeling like something was missing.

I should say this: I've always been woo-woo, if you will. My mom used to call me "Old Weird Barbara." I had three "imaginary friends" and a sense of knowing from a very young age. I have always been told I'm an old soul. I also have always felt angels and/or ancestors around me, protecting me, guiding me. I'm definitely weird by societal norms and have done my best to respectfully rebel against those ideals, but I still felt compelled to mute my woo-woo because most people couldn't handle it.

Enter my dear friend Robin Finney. It's no coincidence she and I met in an online course about creating an online course. Robin was releasing a course/group coaching program introducing others to Oracle cards and I was immediately intrigued. I *had* to join! I felt this inner-knowing rise up within me. This. Was. Happening.

There was more to this magnetic pull, deeper than *just* learning Oracle, it was an opportunity to go all-in on my woo-woo walk. Something inside clicked.

I've felt the pull for many years to embrace my intuition and spirituality and merge that with my design skills. But I would continually stuff that intuition back down inside me because, dang it, design is supposed to be strategic! It must be measurable! I didn't think businesses would take me seriously or think I could actually move the needle for their company if I leaned into my intuition.

Fortunately, that inner-knowing was stronger than my doubts and my spirit guides are as strong-willed and sassy as I am. That feeling was nagging, it kept insisting I merge my innate intuition with strategy and give it whirl. What could it hurt?

I took a deep breath and, as I tend to do when I make up my mind, I decided to go all in.

When I crossed that line of demarcation, so much became crystal clear to me in my life and business. It's remarkable to look back and see how it all fell perfectly into place once I took that first step.

I finally embraced my true, authentic self and became what I call an intuitive designer. I could see my path to success clearly! My first calling was to narrow my focus and niche down to help spiritual, intuitive entrepreneurs, not just the broad label of businesses with purpose.

Next, I invested in a mindset coach. This was a tremendous leap of faith because I had no idea what to expect. All I knew was that my intuition was leading me to my now coach, collaboration partner, and dear friend, Naomi. I learned so much about my own spirituality, the power of meditation, and the importance of being aware of your thoughts. I learned how to confront and grow from issues in the past so I can make room for my manifestation and abundance. I took this coaching program to heart. I was all in!

One of the most valuable lessons I learned from going all-in and embracing my authenticity is that I can show up authentically with my spiritual sisters without having to mute or filter myself. This was huge! I began attracting my ideal clients through little effort of my own! Something shifted, showing up felt easy, and my clients were seeking *me* out! I didn't have to prepare for calls, I learned to trust my intuition and Spirit to show up and guide me. I truly believe this was the breakthrough I needed to accelerate to the next level of my own transformation.

Now, I walk in abundance. Stress and fret are a thing of the past. No more crippling fears.

I'm booked out months in advance, my bank account is growing while my debt is quickly dwindling, opportunities knock on my door weekly, and my clients seek me out instead of me having to spend all my time competing for business in Facebook groups. The friendships I've made by being authentically me and embracing who I am go beyond those connections created in the past. I feel like I've found my spiritual family. I feel like I found what I was missing.

In my corporate days, I learned User Experience (UX) design, where emphasis is on making interactions on a website or mobile app as intuitive as possible. If the user has to think about how to use it, you've already lost them. As a User Experience Designer, empathy has been my number one tool in my tool kit. Strategy merges business goals with emphasis on the goals of the end user. I've since expanded the focus of empathy into every interaction clients have with our business. And I used to think that an empathetic approach for my client's client was enough.

But reflecting on my woo-woo walk and my own transformation, I realized the importance of leading my clients through the process of applying empathy for themselves first, thus building transformation for my clients into my strategy process. It was a powerful Divine Download that brought to my attention that sometimes entrepreneurs invest in their business from a place of lack, not from a perspective of growth or abundance. And it was up to me to help these businesses with soul to align and design their next-level transformation.

For example: Julie hit a dry spell in her business where she hasn't consistently booked clients. She feels the heavy burden of not meeting her financial goals several months in a row and it's put her in a real bind. She listens to the advice of her friend that maybe a new brand, website, or sales page/funnel will do the trick, afterall she's embarrassed to share her site with anyone. But Julie's short on cash flow and afraid to invest in a professional. So she decided to DIY it for now in hopes that this path will take her to her next client.

When we do anything from a place of lack, we infuse that same energy of lack into our lives and business. We're not creating from a position of abundance and we end up staying right where we are, driving that struggle bus and giving tours. When we do this, we're building from where we are now, not from a place of alignment with our next-level transformation in our business.

Since this massive revelation, in addition to the strategy work I lead my clients through, I have implemented what I call soul-alignment into the process where, together, we envision what that next-level transformation looks like. We discuss what it feels like to manifest that abundance and what opportunities it creates. I'm a big believer in if you can see it, you believe it. If you believe it, you become it. From there I help my clients' business look like the abundance they manifest. We create a soul-aligned brand board and discuss what resonates with them most. We discuss what their customer looks like at that next level. It's become a real game-changer, the client experience is more enriching and rewarding, and there's no room for misalignment. Indecision no longer plagues my clients, fear of making the wrong choice is a thing of the past, and because we collaborate on every step of the process, my expertise is seen as a thing of true value.

None of this would've been possible without taking that first step and owning my authenticity. I don't have to hide my woo-woo. I can be free to truly express myself. And I feel supported and divinely guided in every step I take. Fully embracing who I am and showing up without filters has made all the difference in my life and business.

About Barb

Barb is a brand and web designer and sales page/funnel strategist for businesses with soul, helping them raise their vibe through purposeful design. Barb is a believer in the magic of marrying empathy with strategy to create an impactful and remarkable coaching business that attracts clients on auto-pilot. With over 20 years of experience, her passion is empowering coaches and heart-centered entrepreneurs to feel more fulfilled within their business and make a bigger impact by helping more people through proven strategies in brand, web design, and sales page/funnel strategy.

www.infinitybrand.design

hello@infinitybrand.design

FB / IG: @infinitybranddesign

Flame

Healing through Fire

Wendy Lee

"The world needs our healing and healed light to shine, like the beacons we were put on this planet to be, in order to shift the collective consciousness forward together."

Jess Paré

"As a beacon, the message I am transmitting is that whatever you have envisioned for yourself, your wildest dreams of sharing your light with others, is possible. Not only is it possible, it's necessary in order for us to create a world that is healthier, more compassionate, and more connected."

Michelle R. Lemoi

"I have found a way to stand tall."

Aina L. Hoskins

"Be vulnerable and authentic, that will help you shine your light and pave the way for others."

Chapter 7

Life Lessons from a Firefly

Wendy Lee

Waiting for the sun to set in the summer sky felt like an eternity to my nine and a half year old self. I clutched the glass jar resting in my lap and ran my index finger back and forth over the smooth, raised letters, spelling out each one silently in my head, M-A-S-O-N, to help soothe my eager anticipation. As I fidgeted in the aluminum lawn chair, I reminisced about the adventurous day filled with memories of exploring trails in the nearby woods, swimming in the community pool, and eating one too many popsicles, as evident by my blue-dyed popsicle lips.

I had an awesome day with my brother and sisters and things were about to get better.

Finally, as the pink glow of the setting sun turned us into silhouettes, my brother shouted, "over there!" and pointed towards the back corner of the yard, simultaneously catapulting himself out of his chair. "I see one!" he exclaimed as he ran towards the blinking light.

My heart began to pound. I unscrewed the lid, with six puncture holes I had constructed with surgical precision, with a rusty nail and hammer, and carefully placed it on my seat. A scent of sweet vinegar perfume wafted in the air. It was the only evidence of the previous tenants; the bread and butter pickles my stepmother magically made from cucumbers, picked from her make-shift garden.

It was go-time! The humid summer breeze ushered in one. Then six. Then twenty. Then too many to count. They filled the rural Virginia sky, now pitch black and littered with stars. One by one, they illuminated their little bodies prompting a chorus of involuntary oohs and wows!

I jumped out of my seat and ran across the freshly cut grass until I came face-to-face with my first catch.

Carefully, keeping an eye on the strobe-light pulse of the firefly, I placed the jar on the ground next to me and cupped my hands together, creating a hammock. In one swift movement I captured the firefly and gingerly cocooned my hands around the creature. It tickled the palm of my hand as I gently placed it into the jar and covered the opening to avoid an escape.

One by one, I repeated the process until I was exhausted from galavanting around the backyard, and the canning jar was full. Now transformed into a beacon, it illuminated the path toward the concrete back porch, decorated with potted plants of elephant ears and marigolds and a haphazardly rolled up garden hose, and through the sliding glass doors of the house.

The mystery of the fireflies is magical. It got me thinking, what can we learn from their magic and how do we shine our light bright in this world?

Let's nerd out together for a minute. Fireflies are bioluminescent. Meaning they produce their own light from a mixture of oxygen, the pigment luciferin, an enzyme luciferase and an energy-providing chemical ATP. I know a little sci-fi, but stay with me. Uric acid crystals in the light-producing cells act as the reflective layer that helps the light shine. How cool is that? So if we are living the firefly life, we are responsible for producing our own light. Sounds easy enough. But sometimes there are barriers in the way.

How do we figure out how to keep enough oxygen flowing through our souls that we are able to produce our own light and shine on the world?

Those summer days that melted into summer night memories of catching fireflies were priceless. I felt so free and alive and I never wanted the day to end. Not just because of how much fun I was having, but I knew when I walked through the sliding glass doors, and into the house, everything would change. I was keeping secrets, and it was stealing all of my light.

I grew up in a family that seemed to mimic the cast of characters on The Jerry Springer Show. My parents divorce(s), substance abuse(s), death of my mother, blended families, mental illness that led to suicide attepts, wreaked havoc on my family and my soul. But by far the most harmful experience that sucked the air out of me was the sexual abuse at the hands of my father.

My father was a pedophile, and molested me on a regular basis.

I never knew when he would strike. It was mostly cowardly attacks, in the middle of the night while I was sleeping. I would be awakened by his hands tugging at my satin nightgown with a flower pattern and a tiny silk bow at the top. I tried my hardest to build a protective fortress with my hands, but I was no match. I pretended I was asleep; it was the only way to survive and keep me from puking from the stench of Marlboro Reds and the case of beer he drank daily, oozing from his pores.

My heart would race as if I was in the scariest movie of my life, but I could not find the words to yell "Get Off Of me!" My stepmother was usually passed out or too high on drugs to even know what was taking place as her husband slithered out of my bed and back into theirs. I would find out years later that he was simultaneously molesting my stepsister, in the bedroom right next door to mine.

Growing up in this environment completely annihilated my self-esteem, self-worth and gave me very little self-regard. Very rarely did I feel safe, protected, seen, heard or that I mattered.

The fireflies I caught on that blissful summer day and I shared the same fate. In the morning I discovered all of the fireflies laying at the bottom of the jar.

They were dead. Lifeless. Void of any light. Their glowing bodies now looked ugly. Somehow they were transformed into mere bugs, not the superstars they were the night before.

I felt awful. Immediately I thought to myself it was all my fault. They were at the mercy of my care and I blew it. I must have not put enough holes in the lid, and without enough oxygen they withered away in the night.

As I held the jar of dead fireflies in my lap, a deep sadness came over me. I began to cry. I knew exactly how they felt. I wanted to fly around like they did, carefree, shining my light and illuminating everything and everyone around me, but my light was slowly dying inside too. My oxygen was being sucked out of me and there was nothing I could do about it.

Of course my little girl brain had no idea how to process what was happening to and around me. I don't remember anyone saying it's not your fault or you didn't do anything wrong. And so left to my own devices I created all kinds of survival tactics to make sense of what didn't make sense.

There were two paths that I took to survive. Which for the record, was completely an unconscious response at the time. I didn't wake up every morning and say to myself "today I am going to get up and invite all of these energies in my life to mimic the way I felt, because that is what I know." This insight would take decades, and I mean decades, to discover. So in the meantime I disguised my unresolved emotions into two camps. The first was uber masculine. *I will completely overachieve, people-please and prove my way through life, because I feel pretty shitty about myself, and this coping behavior gets me attention, which I interpret as being validated, wanted and needed.* The second was the damsel-in-distress unhealthy feminine. *I will completely abandon myself in relationships in exchange for you loving me and showing me attention, no matter the cost.*

This unconscious strategy invited in a ton of trauma drama. I was like a magnet for dysfunction. The unhealthy feminine primarily showed up in my relationships. The usual suspects of womanizers, narcissists, drunks, druggies, emotionally unavailable and toxic men showed up in my life to recreate and mirror how I felt about myself. And the uber masculine allowed me to work my ass off, put myself through school, and work my way up the corporate ladder, with zero regard to the consequences of stress, overwhelm and anxiety.

It worked until it didn't. It started with a whisper, then a nudge until finally my weary soul knocked me over the head with a frying pan and said, "Sister girl, that's enough!" And brought me to a breaking point.

I was still in my business dress, with the whimsical green and pale pink flower pattern, when I arrived at the entrance of the property. I was swirling in a PTSD soup of betrayal, abandonment, rejection, abuse and confusion, and had no recollection of the 90 mile an hour road trip I took to get there. I frantically cased the neighborhood, trying to figure out a way to get close enough to his one-bedroom apartment, without being discovered. I eventually came across a side lot that led me to the back of the complex. I parked my car, and slung open the door. I waded through the uncut grass next to a house that looked abandoned but wasn't, and approached the fence line. I peered through the slots of the fence, like a nosey Mrs. Kravitz, until I came across the backside of his apartment. There, I found evidence that he was home. The bumper of his red muscle car was parked on the side. I hated that car. The way it looked. The way it sounded. And the way he drove super fast, getting a kick out of how much it scared me.

I found a footing on the ledge of the rotting out fence post, and awkwardly tip-toed my body high enough to peer over the topto get a better look. My hands were digging into the narrow fence line, like a rock climber scaling Mt. Everest. Little did I know, this was going to be the biggest personal mountain to conquer in my life.

I have no clue what I was looking for. I just needed to see his car. To see that he was home. To do something to soothe the enormous anxiety that was welling up inside me. At that moment everything made absolutely no sense. I was completely out of my mind.

The heel of my sensible yet stylish work shoe sank in the mud as I jumped down off the fence. I straightened my hemline and headed back to my vehicle, which was still idling. As I turned around, an immediate feeling of embarrassment came over me. My entire covert operation had been witnessed by three men working on a house across the street. I was so blinded by betrayal, rage, abandonment, that I didn't even notice them, watching me. I slunked back to my car, bowing my head in shame and defeat. As I buckled my seat belt across my lap, I caught my reflection in the rear view mirror. Who was this crazy lady staring back at me? How the hell did I get here? What happened? In the span of four months I went from a happy, productive, human being with a successful corporate career as Senior Vice President of Human Resources to this. I had friends and a fulfilling life and now I was a shell of a person that was in a full blown PTSD panic mode.

Between the flood of tears obstructing my view and negotiating the torque and leverage of how hard I would need to steer to the left to hurl my car over the Ship Channel Bridge, I somehow managed to make it home.

Luckily I'm a scaredy cat by nature, and afraid of heights, so suicide by bridge was off the menu, at least for the moment. And the truth is I really didn't want to die, I just didn't want to feel this deep rejection, again.

I pulled into my driveway, and pushed the button on the garage remote, clipped to the visor. I was completely exhausted. All this PI work was really taking a toll. My throat was hoarse from yelling and my eyes were puffy and burning from the anguish released on my cheeks.

I walked inside and collapsed on the sofa. I began to

replay the events of the day, and the agony of another failed relationship. Suddenly, it hit me like a punch in the gut. For the first time I realized that I was in an abusive relationship, and it wasn't my first. For years I had repeated this pattern. But this time would be the last.

I mustered up just enough snap to remember who I was and what I had learned with the transformational work I had been focusing on to better myself. At that moment, somehow, I could see that I had a choice. A choice to simply take one step. I summoned my muscle memory from all of the work I'd done with coaches and took one action step to get me past this point of no return and back into my body.

I fumbled through my iphone, my hands still shaking from the adrenaline high, and located *Donna Lifeline* in my contacts. "Hello my sweet sister, how are you," she replied.

I was quiet for a moment; it was hard to get the words out past the lump in my throat.

"What's wrong, are you alright?' she prompted.

"I'm in deep trouble and I need help." I quietly said.

I had met Donna a few years earlier at my first transformational retreat. We hit it off and developed a beautiful friendship. She left her corporate life and started a life coaching business, and I knew I could trust her to help me through.

I booked a flight and spent the next two weeks at Donna's house being nurtured back to myself. Morning routines of ginger tea that her husband brewed, nature hikes to waterfalls, reiki, hugs, listening, art therapy, and cry-talking, I slowly found my way back.

This was the moment that helped me to understand my default patterns, and experience the miracle that is transformation; an ability to see yourself differently and make a choice from a place that honors your highest good.

The fact that I was cognitive enough, through all the crazy thoughts and actions, to reach out for help, allowed me to witness and embody the life changing power of transformation and restore my hope.

As I've walked along my transformational journey I carry a lot of life lessons from my childhood memories of catching fireflies.

The Keys to Healing

1) You Are the Gatekeeper (Boundaries and Discernment)

Knowing that you are the gatekeeper of your mason jar is key. Remember the reflector part of the firefly? Think of that as a bouncer. You know that dude, guarding the entrance into your favorite nightclub. The one that held the key to either a night of wild dancing on speakers, or a long wait in the cold in your skimpy Madonna wannabe tulle skirt, pointy neon pink pumps and an army of bangle bracelets adorning your arms. Well guess what, you are the bouncer of your life and have absolute authority in what gets in or not.

Easier said than done. We may not have developed, or know how to access, healthy behaviors; especially if some of our trauma drama is still running the show. Developing, through practice, the ability to execute discernment, that is whose light we allow in, determines whether we brighten, dim or extinguish our light.

2) You Can't Share What You Don't Have

Every single day, multiple times a day, way too many times (dramatic intro I know) I see women leaders giving themselves away to the point of depletion, exhaustion, illness, depression, you can fill in your own adjectives. Why are we doing this? This is not sexy my friends. When we give everything away there is nothing left. Learning to say yes to what feeds your soul and raises your vibration and no thank you to things that feel heavy or drains our energy is a practice that we can not afford to ignore.

3) You Don't Have to Go it Alone

Sometimes our light is extinguished by circumstances that we have no control over. Asking for and receiving support is a crucial component of firefly living. Even with trauma, there is always a little spark that we can grab onto. But sometimes it's hard to see that we need help when we are in the trenches. A trusted life coach, mentor or confidant can help when we struggle to know how to help ourselves—and we all feel this way sometimes. And learning how to access this light is a gift that is always at our disposal. The ownership of this magnificent gift is to nurture its existence. And the best way is to become a witness of your own behaviors and lovingly remind yourself you can choose beyond the automatic survival response mode.

4) Community and Collaboration

Finding a tribe that gets, supports and nurtures you is a must. It's easy to isolate and feel alone, but what I know for sure is that we are all in our little caves feeling exactly the same and sharing and connecting are vital for healing. The days of competition and *'I don't need nobody'* are so old school! Plus collaborating and building community makes life so much easier and so much more fun!

5) Progress over Perfection

Be kind to yourself as you navigate the waters of healing. It takes time. This transformation work is not like a bowl of microwaved oatmeal, where you pop it in and in one minute you're good to go. It takes time and comes in layers. Every step opens us up to the next level and we heal and prosper a little more each time. That's how we grow. There's no getting it right or getting it perfect. It can feel messy and uncertain, but it is so worth it. Show yourself compassion and love. You got this!

Lighting Up the World in a New Way

The world is crying out for healing. Women leaders (that's you) are being called to heal so we can light up the world in a new way. A way that values brave and vulnerable hearts, collaboration over competition, massive self care and mental well being, normalizing, asking for, and receiving help and honoring that which serves our highest expression, so we can be of service to ourselves and others.

The concept of not being enough is a false narrative. Fear of failing. Fear of loving and being lovable. Fear of asking for help. Fear of taking a chance. Fear of speaking our truth. All of it is not true. Listen closely, we no longer have a choice to sit on the side lines. The world needs our healing and healed light to shine, like the beacons we were put on this planet to be, in order to shift this collective consciousness forward together.

Every time I witness women, including myself, staying small because their unhealed trauma is running the show—it pisses me off, and hurts my heart, but mostly pisses me off.

Transforming behavior patterns, that run generation deep, is not for the faint of heart. But staying in the mess of depletion, overwhelm, shrinkage, and not shining our light, is an unconscionable travesty. Not to mention a recipe for crazy making. And I for one am so done with staying stuck in suffering. I invite you to join me in a LeadHERship Revolution! Come on fireflies let's go!

I founded LeadHERship Revolution™ Coaching because I am passionate about leading our lives differently. I want everyone to experience what real transformation feels like in their lives so that others can benefit and be inspired by the spark and encouraged to grab the torch and pass it on to the next person. Our light needs oxygen to burn bright. Choosing what flames the fire is the difference between living the life you were meant to live or being incinerated by the flames.

If your ego just went into protective mode, and you might be thinking *'that may be true for others, but you don't know my story.'* I say, I see you and honor you my soul sister. And what I know for sure is that you can heal and transform your life! The bravery it takes to answer this call is the beacon that shines and automatically invites others to join you on this healing journey. And everything that I am telling you I learned from my nine-and-a-half-year-old self and a few fireflies.

About Wendy

Wendy Lee, influential speaker and transformational leadership coach, was a fresh voice in the world of Human Resources. Having worked her way up from recruiter to Senior Vice President, Wendy allowed her own personal transformation to influence the way she showed up as a leader at work. No longer willing to task and prove and strive to achieve, she embraced a softer, more feminine approach, one that included hearing and sharing her heart. She found leading in this way to be way more effective, and much more fun. Surprisingly, the more vulnerable she got, the more connected people felt, and the more inspiring and effective they were at work and in their lives

Wendy founded LeadHERship Revolution™ in 2018 to spread the message that you no longer need to check your heart at the door to be a strong leader, and that healing and transformation DO have a place in the workplace, and in all areas of your life. She teaches her Contagious Influence approach to women leaders of all ages around the globe who want to Lead Differently.

www.Leadhershiprevolution.com

IG @leadhershiprevolution

FB @LeadHERship Revolution

LinkedIn @Wendy Lee

Chapter 8

Trial by Fire

Jess Paré

Sometimes transformation is beautiful, a graceful unfolding and expanding, and sometimes it's a gruesome, brutal destruction of all that was, a wildfire scorching the old growth to make way for the new.

The winter of 2020 was my latest trial by fire. I have had many such moments of extreme pressure over the past decade, but this one was a doozy!

That February, I had a promising new relationship, was a finalist for several full-time jobs that would bring me financial stability for the first time in years, and I was feeling more hopeful about the future than I had in a very long time. I could vividly see and taste what my life was about to become and I was straining for it, holding my breath until I could finally relax again.

You see, I had been relying on the financial support of my amazing parents for two years while I got back on my feet after relocating and leaving my career in the non-profit sector. I had also been searching unsuccessfully for love and partnership for several years following my divorce. And I had founded and closed my first business (Blue Mountain Life Coaching). I was ready for change. Surely this was my time!

Then, within a span of a few weeks, the budding romance ended, I was not offered any of the jobs I was interviewing for, my therapist and I parted ways, and the world went into lockdown with the news of a global pandemic.

I spent the next few months crawling through depression, anxiety, and hopelessness. Though I desperately wanted to push through it and fake it till I made it back to health, I had no choice but to surrender to the truth that I was not okay, and to seek the support I needed.

Fortuitously, just before all this *ish* hit the fan, I was referred to an anxiety disorders clinic for evaluation. It was such a relief to be diagnosed with generalized anxiety disorder and to begin cognitive behavioral therapy because it gave me hope that I could learn to manage my anxiety so that it no longer ruled my life.

The spring of 2020 was a forest fire that ravaged my future plans and dreams. But in the aftermath of the fire, I learned many essential skills, including:

- To deal with uncertainty,

- To manage my perfectionism,

- To validate myself rather than seek validation outside of myself,

- To identify resources that could support me, and

- To take risks even when failure might be the result.

Just as pyrophytic plants like eucalyptus require fire for their seeds to germinate, my journey to becoming an entrepreneur could not have succeeded without the period of destruction that initiated it.

These skills allowed me to define what success as a

business owner looks like, to treat the process of building a business more like a playful experiment, and to respond to myself with greater compassion when I inevitably make mistakes.

When I started my life coaching business in 2019, it failed within the first month. I attribute this to not having the skills listed above. As soon as things got hard and it seemed like failure might be a possibility, I failed ahead of time by quitting. I was too ashamed to reach out for support and I was crippled by the thought, *'I have no idea what I'm doing.'*

So how did I go from having a panic attack on the floor because I felt like a fraud to running a successful company just one year later?

I attribute it to five powerful practices that allow me to be more resilient, courageous, and bold.

Find Support

In starting my second business, Alchemy Learning Solutions, my very first act as a new business owner was to hire a business coach to help guide me. One of her very first homework assignments was for me to have one coffee chat per day for a month.

I couldn't believe she wanted me to find 30 people to talk to, and I had no idea how I would make it happen or what would come of it.

After networking my butt off and inviting every person I met to connect and get to know each other better, I met that goal.

Not only did this strategy result in my first round of

clients, it created a groundswell of momentum in my business and buoyed me with the confidence I needed to keep putting myself out there.

Getting to know this many people in such a short time also gave me invaluable feedback about how my services were positioned in the marketplace. I observed how people responded when I gave my elevator pitch, I noted what questions were most common, and I used these conversations to inform what I offered in my packages.

The second strategy my coach recommended was for me to join a networking community. She invited me to be her guest at the local chapter of the eWomenNetwork and although the membership fee felt like a big stretch for me at the time, I decided to make the investment.

Joining this group was pivotal to my early success because it allowed me to become part of a community of practice where I could regularly get advice and encouragement from other business owners. There's nothing quite like the support of a passionate group of women entrepreneurs.

If you do nothing else when you're just getting started in business, find yourself a coach and a community of support!

Intentionally Notice & Celebrate Wins

If you've ever struggled with perfectionism, then you know the feeling of hyperfocusing on every little detail that didn't go exactly right. You finish delivering a workshop and have a flood of messages thanking you for sharing your wisdom, but all you can think about is the way there was a typo on slide 4 and how you forgot to mention that essential thing.

Yep. I've been there!

Shortly before starting my business, I decided to begin a new practice that I call the Monthly Badass Review. I set aside 30 minutes to an hour, light a candle, put on some meditative music, and write down all the things I'm proud of accomplishing that month.

This list includes achievements related to my work, my personal development, my mental and physical health, my relationships, and my self-care practices. I don't stop writing until I fill an entire page.

A pro tip is to enlist a friend to do this with you and share some of your achievements each month with one another so you can witness and celebrate each other's growth. It's fun, helps build connection, and gives you accountability!

Reality Check What Constitutes "Success"

With no one as my boss to tell me what the expectations are for my business, I have noticed how important it is for me to intentionally identify what success in my business means to me.

This is so important because in the absence of clear, rationally determined expectations, my inner perfectionist (a.k.a. inner protector) takes the wheel and we inevitably end up hurtling toward the edge of a cliff somewhere in the midst of an existential crisis.

The danger occurs when we aren't explicit with what success means so we end up measuring ourselves against vague or unclear metrics. For those of us with a tendency toward perfectionism, this often leads us straight to feeling like we're just not measuring up even if there's no data to support that.

Another pitfall when setting goals or indicators of success is choosing goals that are outside of our control or sphere of influence. For example, I noticed that early on in my business I was subconsciously defining success as how many products my clients sold. The problem was that I had very little influence on the sales process and there were many other factors that went into determining their sales. In fact, the service I offered was completely on the product development side, not sales and marketing.

This would be like the chef at a restaurant creating a delicious meal but feeling like a failure because no one came through the door to eat it. We all know that it's the responsibility of the marketing department to get people in the door, and that a much more reasonable measure of success for the chef would be customer satisfaction and repeat business but without taking the time to determine for ourselves what success looks like, we can fall prey to this mode of thinking.

So, my friends, take it from me and be sure to determine what winning looks like to YOU! And then recognize yourself for making progress towards that vision.

Cultivate Self-Compassion

Being an entrepreneur is a bold and vulnerable choice. There are SO MANY things we have to consider and learn and try every single day because the buck stops with us. We are the business. This can sometimes feel exhilarating and exciting, and other times can feel like drinking from a firehose.

Think about it...lining your face up with a firehose and turning it on. There are inevitably going to be moments where you choke and sputter and get blasted in the eyeball. In these moments of struggle, or fumbling, or awkwardness, it can be so easy to fall into self-blame and self-judgment. Which—if I indulge it—typically sends me straight to, '*What the hell was I thinking? Who am I to think I could do this?*'

Not the best place to be, eh?

But self-compassion is the antidote and there are many different self-compassion practices that can help remind us of how incredibly courageous we are.

My personal favorite is simple. I tap into my inner wise woman. I picture her as a very old, very wrinkly, very wise lady who clasps her hands in front of her and smiles from her eyes at me. When I tune into what she would say to me when I get hit in the face by the firehose, it usually sounds like this:

Oh, child. You're having a hard time right now. You poor dear. Don't you worry about a thing. You'll be just fine. I know it's hard and you feel lonely and scared sometimes. Of course you do! But I'm here with you.

According to leading self-compassion scholar and psychologist, Dr. Kristin Neff, the three characteristics of self-compassion are acknowledging that you're suffering, responding with kindness, and reminding yourself that whatever you are experiencing is a common human experience. (Self-Compassion: The Proven Power of Being Kind to Yourself Paperback – June 23, 2015).

Sometimes we can find that these are tough to apply to ourselves but much easier when we're thinking of a friend who is suffering. So by stepping into a different persona of the inner wise woman, we are able to turn towards ourselves with compassion.

Surrender to the Unknown

One of the single most powerful shifts I made that allowed my second business to succeed was to learn how to surrender to the unknown.

You may remember that the thought that killed my first business was, *'I have no idea what I'm doing.'* Now, instead of making myself wrong because I don't know how to do something or can't predict how the future will unfold, I reframe that thought to, *'What questions do I need to answer?'*

This thought is filled with possibility. I know how to ask questions! And I know how to answer questions--to do research, to learn, and to ask people who know things I don't.

If ever you find yourself feeling inadequate or unsure of yourself, try asking "What questions do I need to answer to take the next step?" and see how the plane of possibility opens up for you.

Becoming The Beacon

Alchemy is defined by Merriam-Webster as "the seemingly magical process of transformation." If you've ever had a breakthrough in therapy, read a self-help book that changed your perspective, or had an experience that made the world shift around you, then you know how suddenly and irreversibly change can happen.

My current business, Alchemy Learning Solutions, is founded on this principle: that all humans have the capacity to be transformed, and that knowledge (in the broadest sense of the word) is the key to alchemizing suffering into growth.

This is why I work with purpose-driven entrepreneurs to share their wisdom, practices, and techniques with the world by creating experiential and transformative online courses, memberships and programs.

This creation process is truly magical for all involved. Not only does the end user get a powerful experience of learning and growth, but the creators I work with also find themselves transformed by the process of refining their message and stepping into a bigger and bolder version of themselves.

As a beacon, the message I am transmitting is that whatever you have envisioned for yourself—your wildest dreams of sharing your light with others—is possible. Not only is it possible, it's necessary in order for us to create a world that is healthier, more compassionate, and more connected.

About Jess

As Chief Learning Alchemist, Jess brings clarity and confidence to the creation process. She effortlessly draws out essential information from clients to turn disorganized content into a cohesive experience that takes learners on a journey of transformation.

After embarking on her own journey of transformation several years ago, including training as a life coach with the Kripalu Center for Yoga and Health, and certification in Reiki I, Jess's appreciation for the work of purpose-driven entrepreneurs led her to create Alchemy Learning Solutions to provide holistic learning experiences to more people.

Jess holds a Master's of Education from the College of William and Mary, a certificate in Human Resources, and certification as an instructional designer by the IDOL Courses Academy.

www.alchemylearningsolutions.com

jess@alchemylearningsolutions.com

IG & FB: @alchemylearningsolutions

Chapter 9

Be the Light!

Michelle R. Lemoi

"I never wanted you kids."

I heard these words from my mom at 18. At the time, it was like a bullet through my heart. I distinctly remember she was tired and unhappy in her second marriage. I'm sure she was unaware of the impact of her words, but it didn't make them hurt any less. I felt frozen, small, and invisible. I wanted to disappear. There wasn't enough space in the room for me to exist. In that simple sentence, she confirmed everything I had felt and experienced my entire life. A life of unreasonable expectations, lack of a safe environment in which I was able to explore and shape my sense of self, a lifetime of being unseen and unheard, and endurance of 18,000 hours of dysfunction, physical, and emotional abuse.

On the outside, our family life didn't represent any of this view. In pictures, we were well-dressed, smiling, and respectful to all. In essence, we were the perfect family. My parents provided a roof over our heads, food on the table, beautiful clothing, and opportunities to dance, play sports, and participate in anything we wanted.

On the inside, there was withholding of love, periods of silence that lasted for weeks, violent spankings, fighting, manipulation, isolation, and the inability to show emotions. If we laughed, we were too loud. If we cried, we would be given something to cry about. I was at war with my siblings garnering for attention, jockeying to be the favorite, and unable to make true connections to those I loved. There was no individuality nurtured, fostered, or celebrated. My being alive somehow caused discomfort. Always. Signals were mixed. There was always this paradox which led to a very confusing life and no clear understanding of what is normal or healthy.

I spent my entire childhood trying to win over my parents. I longed for their love. I craved acceptance. I wanted to be seen and heard, not invisible and silenced. I longed to understand who I was and what was my place in this family. I became hypervigilant. I was an expert in reading faces, body language, and signs. I became the responsible one, the fixer, the smartest, the goody-goody, and the overachiever. Always, I wondered when the proverbial rug was going to be yanked out from under me. I lived in fear. But mostly, I wanted to escape. I couldn't wait to be 18 and out from under either of my parents.

At the age of 12, I spent less and less time at home whenever possible. I babysat for three families after school, at night, and on the weekends. At 15, I worked in a nursing home as a housecleaner and worked any holidays available as I would rather be with patients cheering them up than deal with the fighting going on at home. As patients died in the nursing home, I was ill-equipped to handle loss. There was no one in my family to help me deal with the strongest of emotions. After a year, I was offered a job as a cashier working for a pharmacist closer to home and I could ride my bike. I didn't want to rely on either of my parents for help. I picked up every available shift and I achieved high honors in my classes. I subconsciously and consciously made a promise that I would not be defined by the chaos of my family life. I would stand alone and pave my own way. I would do whatever it was I wanted to do in my life. I never shed a tear in front of either of my parents. That armoring up would remain with me for years to come.

At this time, my parents were getting divorced. My mom was having an affair. My dad was a mess. I chose to live with my dad on a boat. My role changed to caregiver pretty quickly. What was worse? I was a spitting image of my mother and my dad was dealing with unresolved anger and grief. I was the brunt of those emotions on more than one occasion.

After graduation my story didn't progress like my friends. I didn't go off to the college of my choice despite acceptance. My parents had finalized their divorce and both were in new marriages in a very short time frame. The impression I received was we were old enough to take care of ourselves. Mind you, I was 18, my siblings were 14 and 11 respectively. Because my parent's marriage started to crumble when I was 15, I was left on my own to parent myself.

Armed with little to no skills, I ventured out into the world. I got a job. I started going to school at night and on weekends. I worked for a company that gave me the opportunity to grow, but with an environment that had similarities to my upbringing (this would prove to be a recurring theme in my life.) I vowed to excel and win people over. I did. It was my first experience in the construction industry and I got the bug. I loved problem-solving, the building process, and working with vendors to develop and implement a plan resulting in a celebration of success. This was how I continued my approach through the next 25 years of my construction career.

Each job in my career, I would repeat this exhausting pattern of overachieving, overworking, and burning out. My physical health suffered, mentally I was drained, emotionally I felt like I was on a roller coaster. Inevitably, I stayed too long in jobs that didn't support me and I tolerated behavior that was unacceptable. Some people I would win over, others not. The ones I did not, proved devastating to me. What did I do wrong? Why didn't they like me? I was paralyzed with fear, inadequacy, and lacking self-esteem and worth.

Concurrently, I was dating men that were unavailable emotionally, narcissistic, and alcoholics. On my wedding day to my first husband, I was outside in the limousine not wanting to go into the church. I had suffered emotional abuse at the hands of my soon-to-be husband when he was drinking, which was increasingly frequent. I found myself wondering each day which husband I was going to come home to, and I was told my aspirations didn't matter only that of my husband. My mother told me, "At least he doesn't beat you." So I got out of the limo.

After we were married, I did whatever it took to finish my schooling. I worked full-time and attended school nights and weekends. It took me 4 years, but I did it. After that, my own dreams of advancement and getting my masters were put on hold. After ten years of being together, my needs went unmet. I found out, after repeated failed attempts, that I couldn't have children. On my 30th birthday I blew out the candles on my cake and realized, "There had to be more to life than this." Two years later, I left my husband. I had survived another dysfunctional situation and the grief that ensued swamped me. I was a lost soul.

Living in another state, I looked for any diversion to stop the pain of which I was entrenched. A man walked into my life, paid me a compliment telling me I was beautiful. I had never heard this before. Suddenly, men showed up wanting to date me. My husband and I were separated and heading for divorce. At the time, I didn't understand that I was in a vulnerable state. I didn't know that I should take care of myself, work through the emotions I was feeling, and not do anything harmful to myself. I didn't have any training on how to deal with these kinds of situations. So I stumbled, made huge mistakes, and was very unkind to myself. I allowed others to continue to treat me horribly, I participated in risky behavior, and I did anything I could to be invisible, discarded, and ultimately, further punish myself. I had hit my rock bottom.

The paradox was I was highly functioning, successful at work, and had friends. I had found my best friend, who was a shining beacon of light. I was figuring out my sense of style, I spent days nurturing myself at the ocean, I grieved, I spent every minute I could with my grandmother who was my biggest cheerleader, and I was in great physical health.

Not more than seven months after being separated I had a one-night stand. Several weeks later, at 6 am in the morning while I was fast asleep, I heard a whisper in my ear, "Michelle, you are pregnant." I awoke with a start and ran to grab a pregnancy test. After more than four years of trying with my husband, I was staring at a pregnancy test that read positive. How could this happen? What was I going to do? Good lord, how am I going to tell my husband? Trembling, I sat in shock on the bathroom floor.

The ultrasound confirmed my pregnancy. I believe my son sent me a message in his heartbeat "143." My best friend shouted, "He's telling you I love you—get it?" I agonized over the "right" decision to make. Ultimately, I said yes. Unknowingly, if I didn't say yes, my life might not turn around. If I didn't say yes, I might have continued further harm to myself. If I didn't say yes, would I ever be presented the opportunity to have a child again especially after the previous medical diagnosis? If I didn't say yes, would I ever know what it was like to love another?

Single motherhood was challenging. One of the hardest parts of my life and ultimately, my journey to heal.

My son taught me to love myself as much as he loved me. Every decision I made moving forward, I did for my son. There was much to unravel and life continued to be a struggle. I divorced my first husband, lost the house through bankruptcy, changed jobs, moved, created a steel erecting business, got married again, was a stepmom, coached my son's teams no matter what sport he played, was wildly successful and failed in my business and closed it after seven years, got divorced again, filed bankruptcy a second time, got a job, dated again and then decided I had had enough. Slowly, I was healing, learning, and walking away from that which didn't serve me. After removing the last toxic stronghold in my life, I found a new job working with good hearted people, and I created a new business to elevate women in the construction industry.

My most defining and healing life moment; however, is that I have worked hard at showing up as a loving and supportive mom. At times I have wondered, will I ever get it right?

At six years old my son was diagnosed with generalized anxiety disorder and sensory issues. What I realized was I had been parenting him similar to the way I had been parented where compliance was the key to success. But, that left a lot of struggle, disharmony, and me feeling like a complete failure as a mom. So I got help. For both of us. I learned how to reparent my son so completely differently and it worked. As time went on, my son thrived. He became a leader in school. I accepted him for who he was. He didn't have to wear jeans, scratchy tag shirts, dress up, and be someone he wasn't. We realized we both needed lots of downtime. No go-go-go mentality. We started to travel together and create memories. We learned to laugh, be silly, make mistakes, and keep trying. Remarkably, my son has such a great sense of self at his age than I have had my entire life.

There was no playbook. I definitely couldn't use my experiences as a child as reference for parenting him. I didn't have any role models. Everything I learned was trial by fire. Just as in every other corner of my life.

In 5th grade, the kids participated in a drug free assembly. As parents, we eagerly filed into the gymnasium. I sought out two close friends of mine I met through my son being their son's best friend. As the assembly unfolded, I watched my son with an enormous amount of pride. He was showing up. He was vulnerable enough to sing, dance, and participate. At the end of the musical number, the kids rushed to their parents in the stand and presented them with personal notes. My son handed me mine and said, "I love you, Mom." Tears flooded my vision. Most kids flung their notes at their parents and ran back to the floor. Mine kissed my cheek, smiled, and ran back. As I gently unfolded the letter and browsed the words he had written, an escape sobbed from the back of my throat. I wept. "I love you Mom. Thank you for letting me be me. Thank you for loving me. You are the best mom ever."

In that moment, no matter all the changes we had been through, no matter all the mistakes I had made, and no matter what my life had been for me, I had succeeded in my son never feeling how I had felt and never experiencing what I had as a child. He was seen, heard, and had an unbreakable connection with me.

On my journey to heal, I have realized that everything I do is wrapped around the idea that I don't ever want anyone to feel like I have no matter what the situation. I have worked for companies and made sure every decision I made was in their best interest so they would never have to experience losing a business like I had. When I went for my real estate license, it was because I wanted people to find the place they could call home like my son and I did after my second divorce. When I hold space for friends and support them, it's because I didn't receive that and I don't want them to not experience what that feels like.

As a young girl, I can remember lying in bed and praying to God to help me make a difference in this world. My true original heart knew I was destined to have an impact in this world. And as I fumbled, stumbled, and failed, I was divinely supported to keep going. To believe in me. To be a light in this world.

I have worked at developing, setting, and maintaining boundaries, I have learned deep self-care, I work at accepting me—all of me including my complex PTSD trauma, and most of all I work daily at loving me and understanding who I am in this world. I have identified, even if it makes me uncomfortable, that I have the capacity to make an impact and be a beacon of light for myself, for my son, and for others. For that, I am eternally grateful.

As my healing journey continues, I stand ready to navigate the teenage years with my son. As my teenage years were so tumultuous and misguided, it remains a challenge to be present, find the humor, and allow my son to find his way. I look to forgive my parents as I have chosen not to be defined by the words, "I never wanted you kids." Most importantly, I choose to work on forgiving myself for doing what was necessary to survive. I only knew what I knew.

My journey is far from over. These next chapters of my life are a reimagination and redefining. The beauty remains despite the ugly. I have learned my worth. I have accepted and resolved my shame. I have found my voice to be the light in an industry that needs change. I work hard at showing up for me and for others. I have been vulnerable where there is risk of unacceptance. I work to replace my inner critic with my loving parent. I have found a way to stand tall.

About Michelle

Michelle is energetic, innovative, focused and a results driven professional with over 10 years' experience running small businesses and over 15 years additional experience as an Operations and Project Manager for multimillion-dollar projects. She has proven success in managing diverse, high quality projects; with strengths in leadership, strategic planning and managing change. Michelle possesses an excellent work ethic and has integrity with a passion to grow, learn, teach and continuously improve processes through developing and implementing creative process improvement strategies, managing and sustaining positive relationships; and working cross functionally and collaboratively to improve overall well-being.

Michelle has over 25 years experience in the construction industry with a focus on project management, operations, and leadership. She was President of Lemoi Erectors, Inc from 2009-2016.

In addition, Michelle is Co-founder with Sami D'Agostino in an incredible new business venture - Elevate - Women in Construction (WIC). Michelle and Sami are working to develop a supportive container in which women in the construction industry can be seen, heard, connect with like-minded women, and facilitate change in the industry.

Michelle is a single mom to a 15-year-old son and they love to travel! She enjoys reading, gardening, and cooking. She loves supporting women and having girl-time. Michelle's joys are watching her son grow into his own person and being a good human being, enjoying the beauty life has to offer, and being present in as many of life's moments as she can.

www.linkedin.com/in/michelle-lemoi-06058134

www.elevatewic.com

www.facebook.com/elevatewomeninconstruction

Chapter 10

Reclaiming My Light

Aina L. Hoskins, MBA

I was in my board meeting realizing that I could no longer live a life filled with fear, lies, and hiding who I truly am. I drove home planning how to break free from this prison called marriage.

I made dinner as usual. We ate as a family and I then started cleaning. My oldest son went to babysit down the road, my youngest went out to play with her friends and my middle son went into his room to play video games. I sat at the table with my husband and shared that I wanted a divorce. Before I knew it, he had grabbed me by the neck and pulled me out of my chair. The next thing I remember, my middle son was waking me up and telling me to get up—we had to leave. He had already brought the dog and my purse to the car.

He got me in the car with my husband coming after us and he said drive mom drive. We picked up the other kids and I parked the car and called the police. Both my son and I had several injuries and needed medical care.

Just like that I was a single mom with sole custody of three kids (13, 11, and 8). Yes, my husband went to jail, but not before he had emptied out all our bank accounts.

I thank God every day that I had a great job that paid well

and could easily support my family. My mom came from Norway to help me with the children and the household so that we could try to rebuild our lives. I started my healing journey with medical care, going to therapy, as well as family therapy to help the children.

I knew that it was now or never. If I didn't change my patterns and my thinking patterns, I would continue in this cycle of abuse and continue to believe I somehow didn't deserve anything better. I refused to let these old paradigms continue to rule me. I was born for more and even if I couldn't see it, I knew there was a brighter future out there for us.

I have always been a believer in holistic medicine, so we did many different modalities which included conventional therapy, breathwork, EFT (Emotional Freedom Technique), family constellations, and used Louise Hays' book *You Can Heal Your Life*. I knew that in order to heal from an abusive childhood and marriage, I really needed to dig deep, release, and heal so that we could create a richer, more fulfilling life that we all deserved.

I knew there was a light inside me that I had dimmed. I lost parts of me during the abuse. It was time to reclaim my light and shine it brightly, gather all the pieces of me and become the person I was meant to be—a beacon for women.

I spent years healing my heart and soul. Building up my finances again, raising my children to be loving kind productive humans. It was a journey filled with ups and downs, twists and turns, not to mention a couple detours. Something was driving me—it was my inner guidance system pushing me forward.

As I mentioned earlier, the road hasn't been straight for sure. I was laid off from my high paying corporate job, which gave me the time and freedom to attend many workshops and study with many coaches and mentors. I spent years achieving certifications in Dream Building, Life Mastery, Brave Thinking Masters, and Feng Shui, just to name some. What became clear to me is it wasn't about the certifications; it was about the healing and growth that I experienced. I have always been studious so I love learning. This new knowledge proved to be invaluable for me to grow and shine my light.

It was almost like a path was placed in front of me and all I needed to do was to take one step forward at a time. Every day I focused on gratitude for everything and I made sure to take one action step every single day, no matter now big or small, toward my dream. Every day I looked in the mirror and said, "I love you...Aina, I love you. You are deserving of all the good the universe has to offer."

It's amazing how the universe conspires for you once you create that vision and start moving forward.

I started off coaching women in visioning up and creating a life of their dreams. I then moved into coaching women entrepreneurs in starting and growing their businesses. This was truly fulfilling, yet it was just the beginning. I was meant for more. I became the Executive Officer at Squadron Capital where my focus is on integrating companies into our policies and procedures. We focus on our values, taking care of our people, creating a culture of compassion, and giving back to our communities. Then I had the opportunity to become Managing Director for eWomenNetwork in CT. Creating a community for women entrepreneurs, holding space for their growth, encouraging collaborations, knowing there is more than enough for every one of us. I love being the beacon that can hold the container for your dreams and your success.

Yes, I have a past and it doesn't define me or what I'm capable of. I have learned that the more authentic and vulnerable we are, the more we step into our true selves. Yes, all this so-called "bad" stuff happened to me and I have no shame around it. I am happy to share it with you as I know my story isn't unique to me. If my story can help you shine your light, I am delighted.

If we can all feel safe enough to be authentic, supportive and non-judging, imagine what is possible.

I know it is important for me to be a beacon for women now more than ever. Women's voices need to be heard. We need to link arms and help every woman become the best version of themselves. We are all beacons!

About Aina

Aina was born in Oslo, Norway. She achieved her MBA in Finance and has over 30 years' experience in the corporate world working with mergers, acquisitions, budgeting and administrator for a charitable trust.

Aina has studied with many world-renown teachers and is certified as a Transformational Life Mastery Consultant and Coach, EFT, Reiki, Feng Shui, Kinesiology, and many different prosperity programs.

As well as being Executive Officer at Squadron Capital, Executive Managing Director for eWomenNetwork CT, Aina is a speaker, success coach, Finance and Feng Shui consultant. She is passionate about helping women regain their power, shine their light, create prosperity and accelerate their results, so we can all create lasting success.

Email: ainahoskins@gmail.com

Hearth

Lighting Our Way Home

Robin Finney

"Life takes us exactly where we're meant to go even when the path seems unclear."

Adria Deasy Giordano

"My mother has influenced me in ways she never realized."

Lori Raggio

"Our geographical soulmate is our Beacon! A beacon for light, truth, hope, humanity, interconnectedness, oneness, and unity. It feeds our soul so we can in turn be a beacon to inspire others' greatness."

Chapter 11

Not All Who Wander Are Lost, and It's Okay if You Are

Robin Finney

Sometimes our lights are bright calling us home, while other times they're dim calling us inward.

At the beginning of 2019, I was house-sitting for a friend in Portland and wondering, *"How did I end up here?"* I had just returned from an 8-month soulo journey traveling to 11 countries across four continents. I was without a physical home of my own, had no job, and was nearing the end of my savings. The thought of going back to a corporate 9-to-5 job seemed daunting and like giving up. Yet, the idea of doing something on my own seemed uncertain and challenging. I felt lost.

When you're lost and unsure of where you're going, trust that light will appear to guide you.

I received an email that my future coach, Darla LeDoux, was doing a book study of her book, *Retreat and Grow RICH*. At the time, I had no intentions of being a retreat leader, yet I felt called to sign up. During the first group call, Darla led us in a meditation that sparked inspiration. I wrote in my journal about confidence, solo travel, and groups. I didn't know where this was leading but it felt like something big.

The following weekend I received a download. The pieces

started coming together. I sat in my pajamas on the couch with my laptop and began to write. Words flowed out of my heart and onto the page. I barely moved from that spot all day. I was laser-focused and didn't want to break this flow. As evening fell and the sun began to set, I looked up with astonishment at what had transpired that day. I had created a landing page and waitlist for a group travel experience for people who wish to travel solo and aren't ready to do so on their own. That was the day *Soulo Experiences with Wandering Aunt* was born.

Soulo Experiences would take people on an international journey guided by me where they would stay in a variety of lodging, participate in challenges to support them in gaining confidence by getting out of their comfort zones, and capture their expansion through a VIP Photoshoot Experience. I published the page to my social media accounts and sent out an email to my subscribers inviting them to join the waitlist or share with anyone they knew might be interested. It was all flowing and happening so fast that I didn't quite know what to make of it.

As a visionary, I can see the whole vision play out in my mind and feel it in my body. I see the big picture. It feels so real that sometimes I actually think it's already happening.

With great vision often comes great fear and resistance.

We have the dream. We imagine the vision. It's exciting and feels real. We're ready to go! And then...Fear creeps in and convinces us that what we're dreaming of is never going to work; people aren't going to sign up; or if they do, we will somehow sabotage it and cause it to fail. We'll look like a fool who took on something too big and impossible.

Resistance shows up and blocks us from moving

forward. There are too many details and moving parts that must come together to make it happen.

And sometimes, the vision comes, and the timing is not right.

When people began signing up for my waitlist, it felt very surreal and divine. They were ready for it. But was I? I knew it was something greater than me. What I didn't realize though, was all that I would have to go through to be the person who could lead and hold space for such a vision.

Since I had no job and no recurring income, I convinced myself that it wasn't the right time to offer this new experience. I created a story in my head that I would need to be thriving financially first before people would attract to me. That story would continue to block me from fully embodying my vision and showing up in my fullest expression in all areas of my life.

As Abraham Hicks says:

A belief is only a thought I keep thinking.

A belief is only a thought that I continue to think.

A belief is only my habit of thought.

A belief is only a practiced thought.

A belief is only a thought that I think a lot.

The more we think the thought, the more we're convinced that it's true. So, deep down I believed that until I had money, no one would want to work with me. And even deeper than that, no one would think I was worth it.

This belief pattern took me on my own soulo pilgrimage and

journey to coming home to my beautiful, authentic self.

In May 2019, I took a bold step and signed up for a year-long coaching program with Darla LeDoux to become a certified Sourced™ Retreat Leader. I still had no steady income and was uncertain as to how I would pay for this, yet, my intuition guided me to say, *Yes.* I was ready to drop the story that I wasn't worth it.

In addition to that, I was still traveling all over the world living my nomadic life and continuing my mission of modeling in international photoshoots as a way to support local photographers, designers, and stylists. I took on various contract work and freelance projects to support me in earning some income. I wrote for a well-known podcast, wrote copy and email campaigns for a marketing agency, wrote blogs for my former company, planned trips for individual clients, drove for Lyft (only lasted a week)...anything I could do to bring in income. All the while I was working through so many limiting beliefs around money, abundance, and worth.

During this year-long container, I had many massive shifts, breakdowns, and deep healing which led to great transformation. I got honest about my faith and what I believe rather than what I was taught to believe. I leaned into my spiritual gifts and gained confidence and owned myself as an intuitive (something I never thought I was). I started stripping down the layers to my authentic self and was learning to embrace who I am at my core.

In 2020, I was nearing the end of this coaching program and was feeling ready to lead my first Soulo Experience to Spain. I had visited Spain in 2019 and was excited at the possibility of bringing others with me to this eccentric and stunning country. And then, the pandemic hit. Countries began closing borders and shutting down. My travel design clients were canceling their trips so I was losing income in that area. My contract with the podcast I was writing for had come to an end. I was complete with my other writing projects, and once again was in a position of having no steady income.

I came back to Dallas, Texas where I had lived for nearly 8 years prior to starting my nomadic journey. I moved in with my sister and her family of five and resumed life as a live-in Auntie.

My vision felt like it was farther away than ever now.

For the first time in my life, the entire world was facing the same uncertainty. Many triumphed and found ways to pivot and turn their businesses around into profitable machines. While so many more (like me) were frozen and unclear on what to do.

Without travel, I felt like a whole part of my identity was gone. There was no way I could launch Soulo Experiences now. At one point I thought of a virtual option that I could offer to still take people on journeys through Zoom, but my old limiting beliefs and patterns showed up again. I was on the edge of the cliff again, slowly backing away from the edge.

Life takes us exactly where we're meant to go, even when we feel it's the wrong way.

The only thing I knew to do at this time was tune inward. I focused on meditating daily, journaling, pulling Oracle cards, and going on long walks around the neighborhood. I was so grateful to be in a place where I could still go outside.

Many people around the world did not have that luxury during lockdown.

One morning, as I was finishing my spiritual practice, I looked down at my Oracle card spread and had an insight to start offering Deep Clarity Sessions to support others in gaining clarity and insight in an area of life important to them. And then while on a virtual retreat with my coaching cohorts, I had a vision of me holding oracle cards and a wine cork. That vision expanded into the idea of offering virtual Wine and Oracle parties, which transformed into being called Girls Night Inward.

I began offering these sessions and parties. The feedback was amazing. People were loving it. They were connecting to themselves and others on a deeper level. I had created a safe space for others to be seen and heard. It was so rewarding to be able to hold this space for others in this way. But even with all this transformation and meaningful impact, I was hesitant to market these services. I was afraid of what others would say and afraid that my family and people from my past religious life wouldn't approve. So I kept my marketing to word of mouth. It would take another six months of deep inner work for me to own who I am with confidence and not worry about whether or not others approved.

The layers continued to shed. In the fall of 2020, I was preparing for a spiritual retreat in the Valley of Longevity (a.ka. Vilcabamba, Ecuador). Throughout the year during my meditations, I would see myself in a valley surrounded by green lush mountains. I had no idea where this place was or why I was being called to go. One day while attending a virtual workshop, I heard someone speaking about a retreat in Ecuador. My ears immediately perked up. I messaged Lisa Weldon (the creator and leader of this retreat) and asked for details. This was it. This was the place. I was a *Yes* in my body. I was ready to jump and then, my limiting beliefs around money and worthiness showed up again. I still didn't have a steady income. We were still in a pandemic so the idea of traveling to a foreign country seemed crazy (which was a strange occurrence for someone who had spent the previous 18 months soulo traveling across six continents.)

Lisa was very patient with me as I navigated these mental blocks around money and worthiness. She gave me an assignment to journal about my first experience around money as well as any experiences I could think of throughout my childhood, teenage years, and adulthood. The idea was to look for patterns to discover when I decided that I was not worthy.

I had a memory surface around asking for money. When I was about eight or nine years old, I took an empty instant coffee tin and placed a sign on the outside that said 'Donations.' I then proceeded to go around door to door in the neighborhood asking for change. Pennies, nickels, dimes, and quarters began to fill the tin as I went from house to house. When the tin was full, I ran home with excitement. I couldn't wait to show my parents. But rather than being met with praise, I was met with a look of shock and horror. My parents were mortified that I had gone around the neighborhood asking for money. It was clear that this was not okay. It was not okay to ask for money.

It was no wonder I wasn't making a steady income since leaving my steady corporate life. I was afraid to ask. And if I did ask, I would price my services so low out of fear of being told *No*. 'No' would reiterate my deficiency story of not being worth it.

Lisa supported me in working through this and asking, *"What would it be like to trust your Yes?"* That was the moment I jumped. I said *Yes* to going on the retreat. I wasn't sure how the money would come but knew this was an opportunity to break this pattern and old story. I reached out to my network and overcame my fear of what others would say and claimed myself as an Oracle. This ownership allowed me to ask others to host Girls Night Inward parties or schedule a Deep Clarity Session. I had many say *Yes*. The money showed up, and I was able to attend this retreat.

The process of seeing the light within, causes one to go through darkness in order to discover the light within themselves.

It hasn't been an easy road over the past three years. I've spent countless hours in tears working through old traumas, limiting beliefs, and deep healing. I've wanted to quit many times and give up on my dream. Yet, something greater than me has been holding me and reminding me of who I am.

There have been many times when I've questioned why I'm taking on so many different projects; projects that feel like they're pulling me further from my dream rather than toward it. Pressure from the outside world to launch causes me to pull away.

We have to follow our own rhythm, timing, and path and trust that it is leading us where we're meant to go.

Prior to writing this chapter, I tuned in and pulled a card from Alana Fairchild's *Sacred Rebels Oracle* to ask for guidance about this chapter. Restore and Replenish popped out. This is a card I've known so well over the past year and a half. And this time, the message finally clicked.

You are in need of something so much deeper than rest. You need restoration, replenishment, and revival. This will not necessarily come from lying about somewhere taking a moment out of your day or evening activities. You are more likely to gain what you need by breaking with your routine completely and doing something different.

You need some variety, some spice, some change to bring fresh energy into your body, mind, and heart. You need to restore and revive yourself by changing the usual flow of energy through your being.

There are times in life when you're wandering and you do feel lost. Embrace that feeling. Change up the flow and try something different. It may seem like it's derailing you, yet, it's likely what will bring you back to you and back to you're calling.

I'm ready for my calling now. Soulo Experiences here we go!

About Robin

Robin Finney is an Intuitive and Authenticity guide, Oracle card reader, retreat leader of Soulo Experiences, author, international model and speaker, world traveler, and founder of Wandering Aunt. She supports others in allowing their authentic selves to be seen through Oracle card readings, intuitive clarity sessions, soulo travel retreats, and photoshoot experiences. She believes at the core of being human, we all have a desire to be seen and heard. Robin lives a bold, unconventional life as a nomad. Since 2018, Robin has traveled solo to 20 countries across 6 continents and modeled in eight international photoshoots as part of her mission to support local photographers and artisans.

www.wanderingaunt.com

IG @wanderingaunt

Chapter 12

Finding My Path

Adria D. Giordano, MS

"How are you ever going to find a husband if you keep talking like that?" my mother asked.

It was 1996, and I was home in Connecticut for the holidays. Living and working in Washington, DC, for Senator Chris Dodd, the senior member of the CT Delegation at the time. We were at a neighbor's holiday party and I was defending his voting record. My neighbor was of the opposite party affiliation and was rudely criticizing his voting, his stances on everything and basically him. I felt empowered as I stated facts, explained why he took a position on a particular bill, and was proud to serve his constituency. Then I heard my mother, and felt instantly deflated.

My mother's question brought me back to reality. Well, to *her* reality.

Born in Italy, my mother came to the U.S. at the tender age of 14, not knowing a soul or a word of English. She also did not know her father until she met him when she arrived in New York, as he had left Italy eleven years earlier, as many did at the time, to find work in the "promised land" and make a home for his family. He "came here without anything" he used to tell me and my sisters, but wasn't afraid to work, he said. He was poor, a farmer back in Italy, but was determined to make a better life for himself and his family. He joined my godfather and mowed people's grass. Working seven days a week, he saved money and sent it back to my grandmother. He did this for 11 years, until he had saved enough to start his own landscaping company. Eleven years after immigrating to America, he had started his own business, purchased a home and saved enough to move his family to the United States. I learned early in my childhood the value of hard work, how to survive under pressure, and what it took to not only survive, but thrive. I am the oldest of my parents' three daughters.

Four years out of college and working my way up the ladder, I became the youngest scheduler on Capitol Hill working for one of the most powerful members of the United States Senate. I had just turned 25, and loved my often-stressful job. As a scheduler you are by your Member's side much of the time, scheduling his day-to-day activities. Whether it was scheduling the Senator's time to speak on the floor, vote on a Bill, meet with other Members or reconfigure his packed schedule to find time for him to speak with a Girl Scout troop visiting from Connecticut, I was up to the task. Most of the time, I walked (or ran) alongside him discussing his day and how to adjust his schedule (which I had just fine-tuned the night before) so he could now vote on a Bill or squeeze in one last discussion on a piece of legislation about one of a thousand important topics which came up at a moment's notice. Whenever we passed a school group or family from our home state visiting in the Capitol hallway, he always stopped to chat—that was who he was. A scheduler's nightmare, but I respected and admired his values. He would talk to anyone and everyone, he loved people, and serving them was his passion. Inevitably, I would have to politely interrupt to get him to a vote, an interview, or a television appearance on time.

His schedule was my responsibility, and I took it

seriously. I meticulously planned to ensure he not only met his responsibilities as a public official, but that he also enjoyed a moment to breathe. I carefully calculated each minute, and sometimes this meant working until 9 pm or on the weekends. Since I thrive under pressure, this job perfectly suited me.

I inherited my work ethic from my parents. My mother is the hardest working individual I know. She, and my father. Having three daughters at a very young age, my father worked two jobs to make ends meet, while my mother babysat neighbors' children, and eventually opened up a home daycare, so she could stay home with us. She baked us cookies, created the most beautiful homemade costumes at Halloween and was the "room mom" at school. When my father came home from work, she would leave for her second job at a local retail shop, Sage Allen, in the evenings. She paid for most of our clothing with her discount at the shop, spending her entire paycheck on us.

My parents showed my sisters and me what it meant to appreciate what we had, and how to give back even if we didn't have a lot to give. My father was actively involved in our church's ministry and my mother made dinners for our neighbors and a local food pantry. They were both extremely involved in our town's organizations, school groups and helped anyone and everyone they met. We were lower middle class, had one car, and never lacked for anything. Being Italian meant having a large garden in our backyard, and we spent our summers growing tomatoes, peppers, zucchinis and squash, and sometimes sold it on our street corner from a wagon. My grandparents had an even larger garden, and together we canned tomatoes, roasted peppers, peeled string beans, and made homemade sausage. I can never remember a time not working together as a family. My mother made everything an adventure, even when it was hard work.

As we grew older, I began to realize my mother was determined for us to have something she never had: an education. Coming from a strict Italian family, she grew up without many choices. Having a family was something she wanted, but she has often shared with my sisters and me how going to college was never in her future. It just wasn't something her father believed girls should do. Yet, for us, there was never a doubt in her mind that we would pursue college and be independent. My mother wanted us to take care of ourselves and be anything we wanted. She believed in us. She and my father worked two jobs each to make sure they could afford this for the three of us.

But hearing those words from her at that party so many years later jolted me.

"How are you ever going to find a husband if you keep talking like that?"

She said it, more than asked it, with such authority. I felt shocked and disheartened at the same time. In my eyes, her spirit of independence, which once lived in her, and now in us, shattered. She was reverting back to her father's ideals of a woman. Did she lose her dream? Or did it somehow change as we grew older?

Hearing her words reminded me of the irony of the situation. Working in politics was one of the few places I actually saw women have a voice, even at that time. While a smaller voice than those of their male counterparts, there were nine women in the U.S. Senate during my time in Washington, using their voices and making a difference. Now my mother suggested I not use mine? I had such mixed emotions. I wanted to be respectful of her, of course, and although I did want a family (including a husband), I wanted a career first. Isn't that the American dream?

This is where my mother and I differed. She had her history, and I had mine. She sacrificed so my sisters and I could go to college and have a career, a life outside of what she had. I think, to her, having a husband and family meant independence from her life growing up and also security. She and my father met in high school, and married a few years later. With my dad, she had someone to go through life with. She wanted this for her daughters, as well.

I knew I had to carve my own path. Leaving my parents, after they worked so hard for us, to move to Washington, a place I knew nothing about, was definitely a hard decision. It was a decision I felt I needed to make, not just for me, but for my younger sisters, as well. I know it hurt my mother when I left. She could not say goodbye. But I kept hearing this internal voice, *You can do this. If your mother did it, you can.* Her strength and resilience live inside me. Did she come to visit me months later and cry puddles in the lobby of Russell Senate Office Building Room 444? Yes, she did. Did she ask my boss, one of the highest ranking Members of Congress, *Does my daughter have to live in Washington? Why do you need her here and can't she come home now?* Yes, she did.

But she and I both survived.

I had to stay. It was on Capitol Hill that I found my love of public service and how I could best help people, much like my parents had shown me growing up. It was the perfect place for me to grow and use my education, my upbringing, and to find out who I was.

After almost a decade of working in Washington, I found

myself ready to take on a new challenge: motherhood. I had been married for two years, and was working alongside many inspiring and successful women. And while I admired their hard work and determination, I noticed something. Many of the women I worked with did not have children, or if they did, they did not see them as often as they wished. They simply could not. The hectic work schedule of life on Capitol HIll gave little time to raising a child. The women I knew at the time really struggled with balancing a career and being a mother. I remember specifically asking one of my colleagues who had two young children, didn't she miss them, as she was often in the office early and stayed until 6 pm most evenings. She smiled, and without missing a beat, explained her favorite part of the day was early mornings, when she drove them to school. She would sing songs and take them through the McDonald's drive-thru before dropping them off and heading into work.

I realized then if I was going to be the kind of mom I wanted to be, I needed to be closer to home near my family. Working long hours was fine when I was single and early in our marriage, but I knew I did not want to have to choose between being a mother and climbing the career ladder. I wanted to be the kind of mom who was home when my kids were home, like my mother, and not just have to see them on the drive to school. It was the early 2000's and at that time, that seemed to be two very different paths.

We eventually moved back to Connecticut, as my husband was also from there. We continued working in politics and had a beautiful baby girl the following year. My mother and father helped care for my daughter early on, so I could go back to work, and then when my second daughter was born, they did the same. I transitioned to the nonprofit arena as it was a better fit for my young family. I continue to work for a nonprofit organization and truly love serving people and helping to make even a small difference in the world.

My mother has influenced me in ways she never realized. Her work ethic, strong determination and words of never giving up, digging deeper, and giving 110% helped me grow in my career and make the decision to move back home. And, although our paths are different, a part of me will also be tied to her. I will always be her firstborn first-generation daughter. I will always want to make her proud and show her how much I respect and appreciate the sacrifices she and my father made for me and my sisters.

As I help guide my own daughters through adolescence and adulthood, it's something I think about more and more. How have I influenced their decisions and how am I helping to pave their way? Will they remember who they are and how strong they are? What will their paths be? The world is very different today from when I was living and working in Washington, and while there are still injustices, women now have a louder voice and a seat at the table. There are more choices, more opportunities, and more voices now than ever before.

I hope when the time comes for them to carve their own paths, I am brave enough to say goodbye and let them fly.

About Adria

Adria is a former political assistant, who met and fell in love with her husband in Washington, DC. (It was his laugh that lured her in.) They moved back home to Connecticut to raise their family. Her love of philanthropy and desire to help bring about change led her to work in the nonprofit arena.

Ms. Giordano holds a BA in Communications and Political Science (Simmons University) and an MS in Nonprofit Management and Philanthropy (Bay Path University) and is an active volunteer in her community. She is passionate about writing, having written for CT Working Moms and currently has a monthly column in We-Ha.com. In addition to her daughters and her husband's laugh, she loves her crazy Italian family, her girlfriends and a really dirty martini.

www.we-ha.com/one-moms-view-broken-glass/

Chapter 13

Find Your Geographical Soulmate

Lori Raggio, MBA

Do you believe in soulmates? Do you have a soulmate? Is your soulmate a person, a pet, or a location? My favorite t-shirt says, "My dog is my soulmate." I have two, six-year-old huskies, Takoda and Klondike, my companions who enjoy walking with me daily. I have learned from them to savor the sights and smells and to use all my senses as we explore our surroundings. But wait, you are probably thinking, did she just say location? Yes. What if the soulmate you were seeking is not a human but a location, a geography?

Since the onset of the COVID pandemic, the land/mother nature has been calling us to partner with her to co-create the next level of oneness. As the world begins to open up and social distancing is retracting, more people are preparing to travel to visit their favorite locations or to explore new locations that are on their bucket list. In the past fifteen months have you asked yourself why you are living where you are? Have you wondered where you would live if you could live anywhere? Are you feeling adventuresome?

Soulmates come into our lives at various times for various reasons. Before we and our human soulmate meet in the physical realm our energies have been looking for opportunities to connect. Likewise, our geographical soulmate has been yearning for our arrival. It is possible that we have various geographical soulmates depending on what lessons we need to learn while on our transformational journey. Source will introduce you to your geographical soulmate when you are emotionally, physically, and spiritually ready. Our geographical soulmate consists of soul places that profoundly change our life. The journey to finding one's geographical soulmate is as important if not more important than finding it. The process is one of metamorphosis, a journey of being and becoming and transformation. It is a journey of self-discovery, authenticity, and spiritual enlightenment. What has been your journey so far?

My journey started fifteen years ago. I was first drawn to the desert from the East coast when my husband and I came to visit his family. I found that each time I came to visit I didn't want to go home. We purchased a custom lot in a new planned community, found a builder and developed plans for a home that I was so excited to live in. As we moved the lot loan to a constructive loan the bank refused to provide us the money due to issues with the builder, so we fired the builder and never built on the land. The land for over fifteen years was a financial drain and I consistently was looking for ways to sell the land. It wasn't until I moved to Arizona and committed to a relationship with my geographical soulmate that the sale was possible.

I knew for almost two decades that I belonged in Arizona and yet the timing was not right to move until the pandemic. In December of 2019 I asked my spouse for a divorce, we sold our house in June 2020 during the pandemic and moved to Arizona. As I began adjusting to my new geographical soulmate, I realized that the process was one of peeling away my armor, allowing myself to be vulnerable and to surrender to the illusion of being in control. Sometimes I can't even explain the experiences and feelings I have as I engage with my geographical soulmate. My photos never seem to do the experience justice, even the most brilliant photos aren't as vivid as the memory I have captured in my heart and soul.

A huge part of my coaching journey over the last year has been influenced by my personal and spiritual growth in relationship with my geographical soulmate. This journey has involved radical presence and active acceptance. Acceptance of being with and staying connected to Source, myself, and the earth. I have learned that when acceptance is difficult it is because I am attached to my stories more than reality. The more I accept the more I can explore the possibilities available to me. This practice has greatly impacted my transformation and that of my clients. With acceptance comes spaciousness, increased energy, increased vitality, peace of mind, truth, and maturation.

I was called to the desert for contemplation, wholeness, peace, hope and renewal. Being in Arizona has provided me an opportunity to slow down to remove myself from the frenetic pace I had been living.

Each day starts with a sunrise that is a reminder of a new beginning and each evening a sunset and at times the only description I have for them are unworldly.

Sometimes what I see I need to do a double take to check my reality. Klondike, my husky basking in the desert and content, to fog that makes things around me look like a mirage, to people in hammocks reading among the palm trees. I also have seen black wolves with yellow eyes that are within a few feet of me who simply turn and look and welcome me to their land and then walk away. My spirituality has been heightened in the desert. I became a best-selling author of two book chapters titled *The Unknown is not Our Enemy* and *Being and Becoming: A Spiritual Journey*. All these experiences have brought a different healing energy to my life that then I exude in my interactions with my clients who in turn have experienced transformation.

I have often heard myself and others describe our geographical soulmate as magical, mystical, mysterious, majestic, momentous, mesmerizing, memorable and magnificent. What words come to mind for you? I recently spoke to a friend who moved from Washington DC to Jupiter, Florida, a place she had visited and felt she belonged. Her spouse suffered a stroke about a year ago while in his mid-50's and had not been able to work and within two weeks of being in this new geography his vitals were normal, he was medically cleared to return to work, and he had more energy and additional capabilities. He was transformed by the energy of the sun, warmth, land, and slower pace.

Now, please take some time to answer these questions so that you can gain more clarity about your geographical soulmate.

1. What environment do you thrive in?

    a. Cooler
    b. Hotter
    c. Sunny
    d. Dry
    e. Humid
    f. Tropical
    g. Beach/Sand
    h. Water

    i. Desert

    j. Trees

    k. Seasons

    l. No Seasons

    m. Country

    n. City

2. Where do you feel energized, grounded, intuitive, all knowing in your gut?

3. Where do you feel peace, calm, connected to the land?

4. Where is your happy place?

5. Do you feel curious, adventuresome, and respectful of the land and its inhabitants?

6. Do you feel balanced?

7. While in this geography do you feel your values, goals, vision are aligned?

8. Does this geography bring out the best in you?

9. Can you naturally be your authentic self in this geography?

10. Do you feel you are connected to ancestors from this land?

11. Do you feel an intense chemistry with the land in this geography?

12. Once you are in this geography do you want to stay?

13. Although this is may be your first time in this location, do you have a sense you were here before?

14. Do you have a strong sense of connection, belonging that takes your breath away and you become emotional?

15. Do you feel it is divine timing that you are in this geography? The universe will conspire to bring you to your geographical soulmate just in the right time.

16. Does being vulnerable feel natural when you are in this location?

17. Do you describe this location as a little slice of paradise?

18. Does this geography support you in your growth?

19. Do you prioritize this relationship with your geographical soulmate?

20. Are you your geographical soulmate's primary supporter?

21. Do you feel your geographical soulmate's pain, and do you advocate for its inhabitants?

22. Even though you are excited to share your geographical soulmate with others, are you also protective of this unique personal connection that makes you feel like you are the only person in the world?

What is possible if you are able to visit or live in this geography and have these awesome experiences and soul filled feelings consistently?

Often when I am walking at the lake, I hear people saying that they need to pinch themselves to believe that they are living in this beautiful captivating place.

I would describe my experience being with my geographical soulmate as:

A cellular-level connection.

I am home. I have arrived.

Grounded.

The energetic level is of the highest vibration.

Grateful. Peaceful. Thankful.

The land is my steward, protector, guardian, and nurturer.

Recently during a session with my colleague and shamanic coach, Veronica said that my ancestors are so excited for me to engage with them, they are giddy and requesting that I spend more time with them on the land and that I ask for guidance and support vs. waiting to be invited. They want me to schedule play dates with them especially during sunset.

What is most important in your life and how does the result of being in a relationship with your geographical soulmate support this? What is preventing you from being in a relationship with your geographical soulmate? What stories are you telling yourself of why this isn't possible now? For me it is important to live aligned with my heart and soul and to use my talents and passion to impact the world. I said, it isn't the right time, I am working, and Dante is in school, my job can't be done from Arizona, I don't want to leave my friends, I don't have the money to move, what if I can't find a job etc... Sometimes the universe creates an opportunity for us when we aren't able to do so for ourselves. The COVID pandemic was what created my divine timing to commit to a relationship with my geographical soulmate.

Prior to committing to my geographical soulmate, I was living more in default energy that can be described as:

Fearful
Self-doubting
Analytical
Living in my head
Comparison to others
Constricted
Resistant
Controlling
Proving
Invisible
Disappointed
Muted
Frustrated
Blocked

Now I am living with Sourced energy, and I exhibit:

Heart centeredness
Abundance
Embodiment
Being unstoppable
Intentionality
High vibration
Freedom
Interconnectedness
Dancing dolphin
Compassion

Service mindset
Learning
Confidence
Playfulness
Curiosity
Powerfulness
Expansion
Acceptance
Vibrance
Alignment
Vulnerability
Full expression

People notice and are attracted to this Sourced energy that I exude. While walking at the lake, an older gentleman said to me: "I saw you as you turned the corner the sun was shining on your face and hair, it looked like a halo, mystical and beautiful." Once you are experiencing this higher vibration then you can partner with Source to co-create the life of your dreams.

Recently family and friends have been talking about planning a visit to Arizona. They all have mentioned they want to be in my energy. My transformation and my partnership with my geographical soulmate are visible and palpable to others. When you find your geographical soulmate, you will feel the universe has conspired to connect you. There is no mistake, no accident, and no coincidences.

While in the symbiotic relationship with your geographical soulmate what are you now available for? For me it is:

Love

Connection
Support (give and receive)
Creativity
Innovation
Learning and growth
Fulfilling conversation
Deeper connection with source
Trust, truth, transformation
Living my life's purpose
Soul revolution (mine and catalyzing others)

While in this sacred relationship with your geographical soulmate what are you no longer available for? For me it is:

Being stuck
Self-doubt
Inactivity
Indecision
Fierce independence
Status quo
Misalignment
Over doing
Emotional exhaustion
Scarcity mindset
Playing small
Heart blockage
Constriction
Resistance
Controlling
Disappointment
Scarcity mindset

I have honored my pace this year which in some ways is

much slower than in the past. I am trusting that I will be shown the way, I trust what my soul is calling me to do and be and I understand that intentional bold action is critical to keep the momentum going and to accomplish my dreams in alignment with what matters most to me.

What matters to me are deep, meaningful connections with the land, family, friends, and colleagues. Moving to Arizona during the COVID pandemic has been challenging with respect to interacting with others. The land has been my savior. For the past year I have been able to walk daily between 9-12 miles per day which has kept me sane and provided me a way to interact with other humans in a socially distanced manner. I have felt alone at times and asked my guardian angels for ways to support me in forming new connections. One such time they answered my request the next day.

My 2020 Mercedes with 6300 miles died at the end of the road about two miles from my home. The car was partially blocking one of two lanes on a major road in the neighborhood. I was concerned about someone hitting my car, so I dragged two large cones from the adjacent street that was under construction and put them behind my car to notify oncoming traffic that my car was inoperable. I started calling Mercedes roadside assistance at 8:30 am and looked for a sliver of shade to wait for support. It was already 95 and it was going to get to 108. A vendor was dispatched to jumpstart my car and arrived 90 minutes later. Unfortunately, that intervention was not successful. Mercedes dispatched another tow truck, and I called the dealership to attempt to troubleshoot. The tow truck driver 90 minutes later called to say he was at the location, but I wasn't there. He demanded I get him to my location and when I said I wasn't familiar with where he was and that my phone battery was incredibly low, he said if I couldn't help him then he couldn't help me and he cancelled the service.

Now I was beginning to panic, and I was getting hot and feeling ill. I spoke to Mercedes again and they started looking for other tow truck options. It was at this time that neighbors and strangers started stopping to see how they could support me. Some brought water and others brought smiles, a sympathetic ear and conversation. I realized that I was surrounded by my geographical soulmate, a 360-degree view of the mountains, and my heartbeat slowed, and my panic resided. A woman visiting from Canada stopped and brought me a care package that included water and a banana. I was feeling loved and cared for and hot. Next a police officer stopped and removed the cones and demanded I move my car. I told her my story and how I had been working with Mercedes for over four hours and she said I could no longer have my car blocking traffic, someone had complained. She softened as we waited for the tow truck. I learned about her family, her previous wish to be a veterinarian and how she entered the police academy at age 30. She was my saving grace. She provided me the tow truck company the police department uses, and they arrived 30 minutes later and towed my car to my home. I continued to work with Mercedes and finally after 10 hours and 6 tow trucks later my car was safely delivered to the dealership. This adventure among my geographical soulmate taught me many lessons.

1. I am never alone.

2. People at their core are humane and kind.

3. Persistence and asking for what I need results in my needs being heard and met.

4. There is always a silver lining.

5. Never judge a book by its cover

6. In business, humanity and relationships always trump process and tasks.

7. Shade is critical in Arizona in June even at 8:30 am.

8. Borrow construction cones if you don't have a flair to signal your car is inoperable even if you are risking getting a ticket.

9. Humor vs. anger is a healthier way to deal with tow truck drivers.

10. Always charge your phone before you leave the house.

11. Seeing challenging and frustrating situations with a sense of curiosity and adventure results in a character and soul building opportunity

12. I do not need to know all the answers. I need to take the first step and then trust that I will be guided to take additional steps that will lead to expansion and abundance.

I realized over the past two years that the relationship I am seeking is not human but one in which my ancestors and the land are calling me to. My geographical soulmate is teaching me about connection at a cellular level so that when my heart and soul are prepared for a human soulmate, I will be energetically ready. My geographical soulmate offers me a playground for my soul where I am called to a higher life purpose.

Our geographical soulmate is our beacon! A beacon for light, truth, hope, humanity, interconnectedness, oneness, and unity. It feeds our soul so we can in turn be a beacon to inspire others greatness.

I am a beacon for women leaders and entrepreneurs who want to seek out and cultivate a relationship with their geographical soulmate so that they can be the most expansive version of themselves while creating the life they desire and deserve. I use my expansion magic to help others understand and embody the belief that the universe has our back and possibilities, and opportunities are abundant for all of us.

Using personal connection, curiosity and deep listening I partner with women to create new ways of thinking, new ways of seeing the world based on expansion, vulnerability, opportunity, and endless possibilities. My use of intuition, powerful provocative questions, silence, radical presence without judgement and serious experimentation (play) results in liberation, healing, committed action and transformation.

If you haven't found your geographical soulmate here are some steps to take:

1. Review and answer the questions in this chapter.
2. Visit travel sites and notice what stands out for you, what gets your attention and your heart racing.
3. Talk with family, friends, and colleagues about their favorite locations and how they found them.
4. Join a travel meet up and explore various locations, see what feeds your soul.
5. Work with a coach to explore this dream of engaging with your geographical soulmate.

If you are ready to explore this concept in more detail and would like to begin your journey to finding your geographical soulmate, please connect with me for an initial discovery conversation. I am thrilled to partner with you on your journey.

About Lori

Lori Raggio, MBA, Founder and CEO of Inspire Greatness Coaching and Consulting, LLC, serves as the creation catalyst, soul activist and intuitive transformation alchemist helping women leaders and entrepreneurs remove their armor, find their authentic self, engage with their geographical soulmate, and live aligned with their passion and purpose.

She is a compassionate, innovative, strategic, and results-oriented leadership coach, human capital consultant, transformational retreat leader and a geographical soulmate matchmaker. She is powered by purpose, driven by insatiable curiosity, and guided by Source to partner with women leaders to explore who they are becoming and courageously support them to intentionally impact the world by leveraging their talents and gifts in alignment with their heart and Soul.

Email: lori@inspiregreatnesscoaching.com

Beacon

Lighting the Path

TaShella K. Smith, MA

"On the surface, my story of elevation may look like others who pulled themselves out of poverty and made something of themselves, but it is not the same. All our stories are deeply personal with impact that will influence generations. I navigated this journey with intention, steadfast purpose and the belief that retreating was never an option."

Elizabeth B. Hill, MSW

"Stories and books have lit my way. I am determined to help light the way for others, as others have lit the way for me."

Laura Monk, PhD

"Being the Beacon means being in integrity, so it is important to walk the talk of the work we are championing. We can't just **talk** of transformation: we must **be** different."

Anne Garland

"Keep the faith, be courageous, be vulnerable."

Deb Sodergren

"As spiritual beings having a human experience, I think it's time we start acting like it."

Dr. Davia H. Shepherd

"If we lived in a world where we were all shining our beautiful lights and being the heart-centered leaders we are called to be, we would create a more loving and kind life for generations to come."

Chapter 14

I Was Built to EllaVate:

Poverty to Corporate America

Tashella K. Smith

From poverty to Corporate America, this journey has birthed countless transformations for me; internal and external. Yes, I was the child who didn't realize how poor I was until recently when I asked my mom, "Did we ever go on vacation?" and she responded, "No." I then responded by saying, "Why, because we were too poor?" and she said "Yes!" Both of us bursted into laughter because it was unapologetically true, but more importantly, we knew that narrative was a thing of the past and would never be recited again.

In my early twenties I began to realize there was something extraordinary about how I viewed my economic disposition; I didn't use it as a crutch growing up. Rather, it gave me the fuel I needed to elevate personally and professionally. Pity was not a luxury I could afford; my only solution was to break down every barrier I encountered. It was simple to me—you need help, ask; you don't have a network, build one; you lack knowledge, seek it; you need money, continue to do those things that speak to your strengths and money will find you—and never ever settle! This philosophy assisted in my development throughout my high school years, guided me through undergrad and transformed me in graduate school. This mindset took me from poverty to Corporate America.

Although this philosophy was simple, it took time to master, but my years in college afforded me the opportunity to put this idea to the test. In undergrad it gave me the fortitude needed to not give up, and in graduate school it enabled me to build a support system that was my foundation throughout my academic journey and a huge contributor to my academic success. Professionally, this belief system drove me to blindly connect with leaders and cultivate relationships that would serve me in the short and long term. Was it easy? No. Was I terrified? Yes—and I did it anyway.

So, here's the timeline... I obtained my bachelor's degree in roughly eight years. That's a long time, right? Honestly, I needed eight years to sift through job opportunities and mature. Thankfully, I secured an entry-level job in Corporate America at the age of 23 and they offered the benefit of tuition reimbursement. I leveraged the tuition reimbursement program and finished my undergrad studies while working full time. I took a year off from school to focus on my career, as my goal was to progress from a Revenue Specialist to a Supervisor. I began to cultivate my leadership skills, build my support system, seek knowledge, and I found a mentor. After the preparation was underway, I decided to pursue my master's degree, which I obtained in 3 years.

In graduate school the beacon in me revealed itself. I was seemingly the only person in my master's program that had a background that did not align perfectly with my studies. This made the already challenging process that much tougher. Still, I knew this leadership program would teach me the skills needed to lead people and organizations with my heart, so I pushed forward with my philosophy guiding me. In the end, graduate school took me from a young adult to a woman. I had been leading the way and didn't know, and I didn't stop to take in the scenery, I was on a mission. I moved forward with determination, vigor, enthusiasm, and a desire to learn and grow. Elevation was the driving force.

The natural progression of success has always energized me, the success that you can feel in your torso. It's loud, apparent, reaffirming, and for me, it gives me confirmation. I learned in my most recent years the importance of listening to the messages received from my body.

Have you ever felt confirmation in your body?

Where did you feel it?

I have been consumed by this idea of continuously doing better and being better throughout my life—but I never gave it a name. So, in grad school when I was tasked with creating a nonprofit organization, I was elated to dream up the perfect progressive organization that would exist only to holistically elevate women. During my search to find a name, I was drawn to the word *elevate*, as the word solidified my entire mission in life: to ensure upward mobility in all things. So, I decided to reframe the word 'elevate' and personalize it, it was now EllaVate (Tash**Ella**). The customization of the word gave life to my fictitious nonprofit, but it also gave life to what I had been actively undertaking since I was a young girl; staying committed to progressing, being biased for action, and finding solutions, no matter my economic disposition. This word, which simplified my purpose, would lay the foundation for me to be a beacon.

Looking back, I used to be in awe of what I achieved, but now I realize I was built for this. This is my life's purpose, to be the 'beacon' for my family, friends and bystanders who thought they were nothing more than another page in their family's poverty-stricken narrative. The truth is, my mother and father gave me some of the most important tools I needed to navigate this course; intentionally and unintentionally.

My mom, a fierce and strong black woman, gave me the gift of mental fortitude. She never gave up, regardless of her odds. I witnessed my mom endure, sacrifice, struggle, and still persevere. What I learned in the book of discipline, I learned from watching her explore life, learning one lesson after another. My keen observation would serve as my biggest teacher and the foundation of my success.

From my dad, I learned the importance of passion, determination, and realizing your power. My dad would say, 'the only limitations you have are the ones you place on yourself Tashella' and one day, I chose to believe him. Looking back, I realize it was my dad's utter belief in me that birthed the belief I have in myself. My dad saw me, and this was my reassurance that my options were unlimited. The belief and confidence my dad had in me was contagious, so this quickly went from an affirmation to my truth. Accepting and believing this truth would serve as a necessity as I moved forward in my personal and professional life. Still, there were hurdles I would need to overcome to realize my full potential as a leading force.

Even with the gifts my parents bestowed upon me, I was a young woman that needed to develop in a multitude of areas, self-esteem, confidence, communication, and self-love. I sought out a therapist to sort out my childhood traumas and a coach to help me build through strategic thinking. These steps forward didn't come without their challenges.

Therapy is a big taboo in the African American community, so you can imagine the remarks that came along with me telling family and friends I was actively partaking in therapy. *Tashella you are fine! You are doing better than your peers. You don't need a stranger to tell you about yourself.* What they didn't know was these 'strangers' gave me the tools and asked the uncomfortable questions, forcing me to unpack abandonment and self-love issues and survivor's guilt.

It was extremely conflicting, I yearned for freedom of thought and finances, but once I achieved this, I was troubled by having achieved such success. I did not feel deserving of this access. Feelings of not being worthy to 'sit at the table' was a real emotion for me. This feeling haunted me for years, but therapy and coaching assisted me in understanding these issues so I could create generational change. I grew to realize that beacons must unpack past traumas to create space for elevation. Releasing my insecurities and survivor's guilt allowed me to achieve, lead and inspire, with pure intent.

As for the corporate world, there was also much to learn if I was to succeed. I knew I couldn't navigate this world alone. In my early twenties I leveraged my professors for insight and direction, but as I matured and explored my options, I was granted opportunities to connect with other professionals who assisted me along the way. One of those people was my coach, also known as my strategic thinking partner. She would not only help change the trajectory of my career, but also how I thought about it.

In the beginning, I went from questioning my contribution, identity, and my ability to keep up in Corporate America, to understanding very clearly and deeply the gifts that I possess and how they materialized within my organization. Coaching gave me the tools I needed to realize my contribution; the gift of the catalyst, vitality, guardianship, connection, and the jewel, all of which make up the essence of who I am. Realizing and accepting the essence of who I am aided me in being a transformational leader; never leaving an environment or person as I found them and ensuring that every person I encountered left my presence feeling empowered and energized.

In doing this I created a space in the corporate world that was safe and without judgement, in an environment that could be judgmental and unforgiving. I led with my captivating personality, as well as my desire to connect, learn, and grow. I inspired not only my peers, but bosses as well. I vividly remember my boss saying I would be her boss one day, at the age of 27-years-old. This belief reminded me of the belief my father had in me as a child, and the impact was the same. Her belief in me empowered me to continue pushing forward.

As anticipated, there was a point in my career where every philosophy I depended on my entire life was tested. At one point in my career, I had to make a critical decision to leave a department I was initially drawn to. Leaving the department meant possible backlash, chatter, and potential long-term assumptions regarding my competence. Still, I made one of the hardest decisions of my life, I left the department and returned to my previous role.

I did not know the impact this choice would have on how I was viewed by my peers, onlookers, or the organization, even still, I had to follow that feeling in my torso, the confirmation from my body. Ironically, after speaking with my peers and reflecting on my decision, I realized what I did.

I made space for one to have complete control of their corporate narrative, without fear of judgment. I inspired others to own their trajectory, even if it meant taking a step back to ensure they were taking the right steps forward. This moment unleashed unknown confidence within me and redefined how I viewed success, stature, and impact. I had the power, the perspective, the guts to do what was right for me and stand in my truth; it was the most powerful beacon move I have ever made.

On the surface, my story of elevation may look like others who pulled themselves out of poverty and made something of themselves, but it is not the same. All of our stories are deeply personal with impact that will influence generations. I navigated this journey with intention, steadfast purpose and the belief that retreating was never an option. Elevating became and still is my life's purpose, but not for me alone, for my family, friends, and peers. I did the work of paving the way so that I could inspire the uninspired and empower the hopeless. I became the beacon so they could see the beacon within themselves.

Today, I am the originator of EllaVate, a business in the making, that will exist to support people in their journey to self-betterment. I am also a Supervisor of a fortune 500 company that has allowed me to be the beacon for people who aspire to lead and or grow within their career.

About TaShella

Tashella K. Smith, creator of EllaVate, LLC., and native of Baltimore, serves as a leader and influencer as she supports women in their journey to unveil the best parts of themselves.

She is an enthusiastic, results-driven leader that has a bias for action. Her philosophy of elevation has fueled her life's purpose to empower and connect women as they pursue self-betterment, seek to find their purpose, and break down generational barriers.

Chapter 15

Illuminating a New Path

Elizabeth B. Hill, MSW

I was 18 and I was a year out of high school. I was very excited to be receiving a book. It was wedgewood blue with silver writing on it. The book was "Shining as Illuminators in the World" and it was published by the Watchtower Bible and Tract Society.

Only people that had survived a year of full-time ministry as one of Jehovah's Witnesses got this honor. We were called "pioneers," spending an average of 90 hours a month out in the field ministry. We received this book for what was called "Pioneer School," where we received two weeks of training in the field ministry and how to be a good servant of God in the world.

I had spent my senior year in high school as an auxiliary pioneer, spending 60 hours a month in the ministry. After I graduated, I became a pioneer. I worked part-time at an optometrist's office. When I wasn't doing that, I was knocking on doors, talking about a paradise on earth, and announcing Jehovah's Kingdom. When we got magazines to hand out that had pictures of Armageddon or the book of Revelation on the cover, I was not so much of a fan. When the cover was of nice and happy people in paradise hanging out with Giant Pandas and Lions, living together in peace, I was ecstatic. Thank God! (Literally.)

To think this was who I was then is so very bizarre to me.

It feels like I was a completely different human. And yet, there I was. I wanted to serve Jehovah. I ached to make him happy.

But the truth was, I hated going door-to-door. It was terrifying. Only lonely people in their 70's or 80's were happy to see me. Most people hid, which would give us a laugh, because we could often see them hiding behind their curtains. Others dismissed us, some politely, some not. From a young age I had been yelled at, called names, sworn at, and had people show up as naked at the door because they thought it was funny. (Fortunately, I come from a family of artists, so nakedness ain't no thing. I would laugh and just thought they were ridiculous, rather than being permanently scarred.) I once had a gun pulled on me. I don't actually *remember* having a gun pulled on me, but I've been told by multiple people it happened. My sweet little mind has a kind habit of erasing the things that could disturb me. Yes, this is a thing, and totally diagnosable, and I got my Bachelors in Psychology and my Masters in Social Work to understand it more. Rather than be upset by this phenomenon, I thank the mind for this service. How kind of it to not let me remember.

There's something energizing about getting screamed at. And getting to feel put upon and RIGHTEOUS. I developed a fierce, burning fire, probably further ignited by coming of age in the 1990's—the angsty time of Smashing Pumpkins, Alanis Morrisssette, Rage Against the Machine, and Garbage. I grew fierce and fiery. I hated going door-to-door, but it seemed to be the only way to make God happy and I was very much wanting to make God happy.

The first milestone as a witness is to become a "publisher," which means you can go door-to-door, speak with people about Jehovah's Kingdom, and distribute literature. The year I felt most pressured to become a "publisher" and speak at doors, I was nauseous, I had difficulty sleeping, I developed severe Obsessive Compulsive Disorder (OCD), and slept only a few hours a night. I started bringing Tums to school to try to calm my anxious stomach, regularly crunching on them in class.

If someone asked me what was wrong then, I couldn't have told them. I would have said, "nothing is wrong with my life other than the fact I'm a horrible person."

I hated who I was. I felt unworthy of breathing air. I was pretty sure God was just going to strike me down with a thunderbolt at any moment.

I want to just go back and give that poor girl a hug. That poor girl who literally did nothing wrong that wasn't in the normal range of being a slightly annoying pre-teen human. In 8th grade, God saw I was having a really rough time, and gave me an English teacher. He walked on desks, encouraged our creative writing, and our humanity. When we were asked to write our names on index cards on the first day, I wrote "Elizabeth or Liz." He called me "Or" for the whole year. I had a new devotion: writing. And I began to recover my soul and health.

When I was 20 I had a crisis of faith, left the religion, lost all of my friends except for my boyfriend, and had a complete nervous breakdown.

I have no bad things to say about Witnesses as a whole. They are generally kind and loving people that do good in the world without fanfare or spectacle. Being there, however, was deeply bad for my mental and, by extension, physical health. I acknowledge that for someone else this same place could be a true haven and refuge.

After a summer I call the "gin and tonic summer," which I hilariously really only remember laying by a pool at my new home at my grandma's despite working full-time, I started at a new school, Central Connecticut State University, and met some of my dearest friends. I was welcomed into the arms of the theatre. I devoted myself to the theatre gods, spending all free hours there, as I had devoted myself to the religion. I was still serving God, I just wasn't sure he was a big guy in the sky that didn't think gay people should be gay. I had also started having a bit of an issue with this whole can't-have-sex-without-a-ring-on-it thing. What the heck? I had a few questions.

I continued to feel this fire. I was here on earth on a MISSION. When 9-11 happened, my flame turned into a roaring bonfire. I remember walking into my "Theatre About AIDS" class at Central CT State University and learning a plane had hit the towers. The day became a blur—were we supposed to go to classes? Or not? I chose not. I was in someone's (??) dorm room watching tv when the plane hit the second tower. I had to do something.

My dear friends Gabriella Campos and Melissa Nocera and I organized a vigil on campus, because we could smell hatred arising and we didn't want war. A large crowd gathered. At a state school where people mostly didn't care about such matters, we were floored by the crowd. We started CCSU4Peace and used art to shake things up and cultivate peace. I mourned the loss of those that died and I sought to understand the attackers.

9-11 turned me into an organizer and peace activist. I wanted to change the world. I got my Masters in Social Work in Community Organization. I went to work for nonprofits with missions to eliminate poverty and make the world a better place. Also, I had babies. They are excellent human beings, if I do so say so myself, bringing light into the world in their own unique ways.

Now I'm a different kind of "publisher" and a different kind of "pioneer." I help people write and share their stories and help people publish their books. Books and writing have been a respite for me and have lit my path forward. There have been times when all I felt I had in the world was a book. Writing has helped me get through things that seem unimaginable—and helped me light my own path forward when the future seemed impossible or unclear. After helping over 80 people become published authors, I know the healing power of writing and sharing your story. So, yes, I am actually a "publisher"— a kind that I'm thrilled to be, rather than doing because I "have to." I continue to feel like I'm on a divine assignment. I would never have dreamed this path for myself. But people/the universe asked me to do it, and I could, and I did. And I love it.

In this new genre of independent publishing through the magic of print-on-demand platforms, I also get to be a "pioneer," paving the way for authors that would have had to wait years seeking agents and publishers. We no longer need to wait on others' timelines and whims to get published. The world doesn't have time for that! When I witness a light, a beacon, I can help them shine their light swiftly. The world is aching for the healing power of story. Many feel lost and are seeking a path forward. Stories and books have lit my way. I am determined to help light the way for others, as others have lit the way for me.

The way we carry light may shift and evolve. My dear

friend and coach Kathleen Troy has formed a group called the Coddiwomple Society. To Coddiwomple is to "travel purposely towards an as-yet-unknown destination." Sometimes, we don't know where we're going, but we know it is very important that we move forward. We hold our light, even if we are shaking in our boots when we do so. We take that next step. The universe has more in store for us than we can ever see for ourselves.

About Elizabeth

Elizabeth B. Hill, MSW is the CEO and founder of Green Heart Living and Green Heart Living Press. She is the best-selling author of *Embrace Your Space, Success in Any Season, The Great Pause: Blessings and Wisdom from COVID-19, Love Notes: Daily Wisdom for the Soul,* and *Green Your Heart, Green Your World: Avoid Burnout, Save the World and Love Your Life.*

Elizabeth coaches clients on mindful leadership and writing to heal, inspire, and grow their impact in the world. Trained as a social worker, yoga teacher, and ontological coach, she weaves creativity, spirituality, and mindfulness into her work with clients. With over 15 years of experience writing and leading collaborations in the nonprofit sphere, Elizabeth brings a uniquely engaging approach to collaborative book projects. Elizabeth lives in a historic (and hysterical) home in Connecticut with her children Raven and James.

www.greenheartliving.com
www.greenheartlivingpress.com

Chapter 16

Shine Your
Maga Healing Light

Laura Monk, PhD

Over millennia, in diverse cultures around the world, women have come together—traditionally, in circles—to share, teach, listen, and learn. Older women were customarily revered for their wisdom and experience as respected guides and healers; they still are in some tribes and villages around the world, although this is not the tradition it once was. In ancient times, before our current patriarchal system, we worshipped the Goddess and Mother Earth; we saw the Divine Feminine as the Ultimate Creatrix.

For some time now, in the turn away from patriarchy, women of all ages are being called to reconnect to the Sacred and feel the pulse of the Goddess that beats within. Around the world, although many small sectors of women have continued to honour womanhood, this is now increasing and gaining momentum. This has been especially noticeable during the Coronavirus pandemic as people are rejoining Nature and re-evaluating what is important in life. Greater numbers of women are reconnecting with the seasonal and cyclical aspects of womanhood, conducting rites of passage ceremonies and initiation rituals, reclaiming Goddess archetypes and tapping into the Collective Womyn-Wisdom.

Personally, I received that call when I was in my fifties

after my second husband left me for a younger woman. Although harrowing at the time, I had no idea that this would be a portal to my empowerment and transformation: as Goddess, Tantrika, Creatrix, and Maga Healer. At the time of this devastation, I was also going through the menopause that, viewed through a patriarchal lens, is seen as the end of a woman's useful life. However, from a feminine perspective, I related to the Maga in her autumn phase and saw that I had entered the second half of my life, rather than being at the end; there were bountiful gifts to come and I had much to harvest.

If you are familiar with the Maiden, Mother, Crone of the Triple Goddess form and are at the midlife juncture, you may be delighted to learn that you are no longer forced into wisened cronedom in midlife, especially if you still feel young and are just beginning to find out who you really are.

Thankfully, the formidable shamanic midwife and self-subscribed, Agent of the Goddess, Jane Hardwicke Collings, conceptualised a *Four Phase Feminine Way*[1] comprising Maiden, Mother, Maga, Crone, which postpones those crone years until we are about 70 plus, and introduces the Maga at midlife, around 50 years at menopause. Hardwicke Collings explains that in the ancient time of the Triple Goddess, girls and women "had babies at 14, were grandmothers at 30 and dead at 45" (Ibid). The seasons of this tri-fold life were truncated during the mother phase who represented both summer and autumn. More pleasingly, the *Four Phase Feminine Way* allows each phase its own season in addition to rites of passage thusly: Maiden, spring, menarche; Mother, summer, childbirth; Maga, menopause,

---

[1] Hardwicke Collings, Jane (2006) *Introducing Maga*, PDF available from https://janehardwickecollings.com/introducing-maga/

autumn; Crone, retirement, winter.

Maga is a truly magical phase of a woman's life. Etymologically, the word comes from the Latin, *magus*, meaning magician: translating for women as sorceress, witch, healer, enchantress, etc. Scholars and ethnologists have identified the term Maga as one that denotes those who practice white magic and healing.[2] It is no coincidence that this term is surfacing now during the turn away from patriarchy and towards the feminine wisdom that Mother Earth is crying out for. The Maga brings compassion, interconnection, intuitive healing and much needed mentoring and support to those in her community who are guided by her profound wisdom and magical gifts. The Maga is like a lighthouse who leads those seeking direction to find their bearings and, when she leads, her love and light aims explorers toward an assured future, which is often drawn from her own experiences. It is my personal understanding that the Maga has a particular gift of illumination to women seeking guidance in the second half of their lives because that is where she resides.

The little known Maga phase of a woman's life encompasses a time of many changes such as divorce, separation, children leaving home, changing or ending careers, moving home or country. As women experience these life transitions, they can gain empowerment, strength and wisdom and go on to become mentors and supporters in their communities. Women can also find this time lonely, frightening, depressing and disempowering when they internalise cultural messages that suggest their life is over: that they are undesirable and unwanted, and have outgrown

---

[2] Leland, Charles, G. (2010) *The Man and the Myth*, OakChylde Publications/Lulu Press Inc, p.148

their usefulness. Truthfully, menopause can be the doorway to a world of opportunities, but we don't hear so much about this version of middle age. When I found myself alone once more in the world, post-divorce (twice) and post-menopause (early), I was forced to reevaluate my life. I was, at that time, immersed in a dry and scientific world of academia and knew nothing of the magnificent Maga, let alone the mystical and sensual teachings I was about to be gifted through Taoist and Tantric teachings. Today, it is my view that the empowerment and transformation available to midlife women can be greatly enhanced by reconnecting to the power and energy of our authentic sexual and sensual selves: that wild, primal, and natural part of us that is connected to Mother Nature and the Universe.

One of the many gifts in store for me as I went boldly alone into midlife, was the discovery of orgasmic and ecstatic sex in my fifties. This was terrifically surprising and took me in a new direction altogether: on a spiritual path, which was also unexpected. I had long had the idea from images in literature that sexual intimacy could be beautiful and profound, but I had not experienced this for myself. I was very familiar with abusive and degrading sex that left me feeling hurt, humiliated, worthless and shamed, and I also knew safe and secure but, ultimately, boring 'vanilla' sex. I did not even think I would have a sex life at all post-menopause as I had endured a sexless marriage for many years and had deeply grieved the loss of my fertility, youthfulness and any evident sexuality.

The lover I fell into the arms of when my second marriage ended, woke up my body and made me feel alive and young again. We enjoyed intimacy in outrageously blissful and connected ways, which was different to anything I had ever known. Where had he been all my life? I couldn't quite believe my hitherto lack of awareness about the pure joys of great sex: I, literally, kept pinching myself. I had seen and read portrayals of ecstatic sex and mind-blowing orgasm in literature and film, but it just hadn't been my experience and, when I was a young woman, I gradually began to accept the words of my first husband on intimacy, "That's not real life – you need to get your head out of books and wake up to reality." Yet, deep inside, I could sense my sexual vibrancy like a diamond buried deep under layers of darkness that I simply did not know how to excavate. I have since understood these layers to be familial, societal and cultural programming, imprinting and conditioning, which we all have to some degree. For the older woman, there is an extra layer that, when it comes to her sexuality, can seem too frightening, risky or impossible to shift. The truth is, that any woman can shift this layer and the Maga knows how.

As a sex, love and relationship coach, I stepped into a Maga Healer role: specialising in reconnecting older women to their sexuality and moving through obstacles to their desires. Using a Tantric approach combined with neuroscience that targets the unconscious, thus combining modern and ancient healing methods, I guide women (and couples) wanting sexual reconnection through somatic practices to reignite, empower and liberate. No matter their age or background, I see that their greater sexual connection and alignment is reflected in all areas of women's lives including family and business. I came to this profession late in life and it is my favourite one yet as it is, not only rewarding and joyful, but truly life-changing. Already a seasoned psychotherapist, I cut my teeth as a coach working with other practitioners, consultants, healers and Tantrikas through my *'love sexy'* retreats that focused on the sexually loving aspects of self-care. Sensual freedom, erotic potential, and sexual authenticity are rarely mentioned in advice on self-care, self-love and self-worth even though sexual energy is a life force and extremely precious. The Ancient Taoists practised the cultivation of sexual essence due to the belief that sex is sacred and that sexual energy has real potency for health and wellbeing: tapping into this energy can generate considerable personal power in all areas of living.

Tantra teaches us that our sexuality is a sacred aspect of ourselves, our lives and our relationships: including that with the Universe, Spirit or our Higher Power. Through sexual experience we can be at one with the Cosmos and this is what led to my own spiritual awakening that I am so grateful for. I have felt the magical power of this most fully through sex magic, which can be used to manifest in a divinely potent way and is a particularly powerful practice for midlife women looking to create something of significance in the second half of their lives. This is especially true for women wishing to reconnect with their sensual nature and be their authentic sexual selves, as the process can be used to create a desired experience around ageing and make it a reality. Similarly, for those seeking sexual healing and working through sexual blocks, the potent trio of sexual self-care, self-love and self-pleasure are key, particularly for all of us lighthouses who want to keep our lights shining.

Working with other practitioners, it quickly became apparent to me that many guides for others have: a) obstacles relating to sex and sexuality that are stymieing their own practices, and b) unawareness of how being cut off from our sexual centre denies the body's intelligence: as energy, wisdom and guidance. For many of us, our magic is in our senses and sensuality, but we have been told not to trust these intuitive and potent gifts. In the patriarchy, science rules supreme and, although we will no longer be burned at the stake for magic that relies on our senses, we may still be persecuted by those with misogynistic, anti-sexual obsessions. Importantly, shame relating to our sexuality that we may have internalised from cultural groups such as families, friendships, religious sects and other organisations, can shut us off from this beautiful, magical and powerful aspect of ourselves that goes beyond the accepted sanitised version peculiar to each group. Sensual pleasure, sexual energy and orgasmicness truly are medicine and powerful healing modalities, yet where can we talk about these innate gifts that are our birthright? How tragic to suppress this magic because of the current world view of sex as dirty, sinful and some kind of evil, rather than a blessing from Source that is beautiful and healing when consensual and conscious.

One of many problems with a sex taboo society is that we are not having real conversations about the aspects of ourselves as sexual beings, so we are not even awake to our erotic potential. If we lived in a world where we understood that sex is actually sacred and that our bodies truly are temples, then we would be able to grow our gifts and greatest pleasures from a young age without our shaming culture repressing our sexuality. Rather than worrying about what we look like without our clothes on, we might ask, am I tapping into the magic that is available to me sexually—and, if not, why not? Sex has the capacity to be so deep, meaningful and fulfilling, yet often we are only just touching upon the possibilities. Tantric sexuality can give us the depth of experience that the mind, body and soul yearn for.

The beauty and potency of Tantra captivated me and I became fascinated with it—setting off down a spiritual path to learn as much as I could about this subject. First, I joined a wonderful women's programme in the UK with Shakti Tantra,[3] which inducted me into ancient teachings and practices. Later, I studied as a VITA™ (Vital and Integrated Tantric Approach) coach with legendary Tantra teacher, Layla Martin, whose training[4] opened my eyes to a whole new way of looking at sex. I learned that the application of Tantric philosophy to sexuality can lead to profoundly spiritual states. This was a revelation to me and totally validated my intuition, which had led me to the training in the first place at Layla's Tantric Institute of Integrated Sexuality. It was not until after I had graduated and begun my extra majors in Tantric Sex and Life Transitions that I learned of the seasonal/cyclical aspects of womanhood and sexuality and was introduced to the Maga Healer. When Layla described this archetype of woman in the autumn of her life, I heard myself reflected back at me. Here was a role I could embody in order to shine my light outwards to older women seeking guidance around sex and sexuality.

Although the Maga is a beacon for others, there is also much inward energy during this middle phase of life and there is both external and internal work to do on the Self. Whilst training as a sex, love and relationship coach, I was confronted with my own discomfort and wounding relating to being my authentic sexual self and I undertook deep inner work, returning to therapy to revisit early traumas. Being the

---

[3] Shakti Tantra (2021) *Women's Programme*,
https://shaktitantra.co.uk/courses/womens-programme/
[4] Tantric Institute of Integrated Sexuality (2021) *The VITA™ Sex, Love and Relationship Coaching Certification*,
https://laylamartin.com/programs/2022-vita-coaching-certification/

Beacon means being in integrity, so it is important to walk the talk of the work we are championing. We can't just *talk* of transformation: we must *be* different.

With much sorrow, I made a monumentally hard decision when I chose to end a relationship that was no longer working for me. As much as I loved this beautiful soul, I knew that I could not stand in my truth with him and, this time around, it was my turn to leave. I have learned, not only, the importance of open and honest communication in relationships, but also the applications of those same qualities for myself for the sake of authenticity: to know myself, own myself and be myself.[5] So, I prioritised my needs and honoured my inner knowing to move on; this was the first decision I had ever made that was completely for me— without taking anyone else into account.

I learned one of life's painful lessons described so well by Heidi Priebe: you should choose the lifestyle you want over the person you want. In her excellent publication, *This Is Me Letting You Go*, Heidi explains: "Picking the person you love over the life that you want means your sense of self-worth will slowly degrade and deteriorate over years of contentedly slipping into bed beside someone you're comfortable with."[6] It is no easy undertaking to leave the person you love, especially when it seems easier and safer to stay. Today's midlife woman, seeking both sexual liberation and transformation needs real commitment to honour herself and break free from ideas of how an older woman "should" behave in her sexuality according to eons of female

---

[5] Joseph, Stephen (2016) *Authentic: How to be yourself and why it matters.* Piatkus: London
[6] Priebe, Heidi (2016) *This Is Me Letting You Go.* The Thought and Expression Company, p.23

oppression: both from external sources and that which has become internalised.

The Maga will be menopausal or post-menopausal, and Collings[7] describes how the main issues with this phase of women's lives revolve around "our bodies, our sexuality and libido, our mind, moods, beliefs, fears, and grieving for what now will never be." Yet, the author sees that many women are now reclaiming their menopausal experience. I concur and believe that we bypass our sexual nature at our peril. Tantric practices such as connected breathing into the pelvic bowl at the area of the sacral or second chakra can not only rewire us to our sexuality and emotional regulation, but also to our creativity.

Learning how to love our selves and bodies, and how to (re)connect to our sexual energy and life force can be truly transformative when we realise our desires and create new realities. No matter what your age, body shape/weight or relationship status, your sexual energy is a potent life force that you can tap into to re-energize your sensuality, personal power and creative fire. No, you are not too old! If you are at the autumn of your life, why not try on the role of Maga Healer for yourself or seek out some guidance to assist you with new vision, purpose and inspiration? You are whole, perfect and Divine just as you are, and the world is waiting for your wisdom, healing and magical gifts. I invite you to speak to your Inner Feminine or Goddess and ask her what it is that she desires around sex and sexuality. For, no matter

---

[7]. Hardwicke Collings, Jane (2015) *Autumn Woman, Harvest Queen*, PDF available from
https://janehardwickecollings.com/autumn-woman-harvest-quee
n/

what your circumstances, the sensual woman lies waiting within to be fully expressed, and you might be surprised to find that she has the answers you have been seeking in life.

About Laura

Laura Monk is a certified VITA™ Sex, Love and Relationship Coach, certified Sourced™ Retreat Leader, counsellor and psychotherapist, and social psychologist. Originally from London, England, she celebrates being location independent in her work online and on retreat. Laura appreciates knowledge gained from Western academia and science as well as teachings and experiences from the Eastern traditions and women's ancient healing practices. Straddling this divide, Laura identifies as Goddess, Tantrika, Creatrix and Maga Healer, with a PhD in Psychology and Behavioural Science, a Master of Science in Psychology from Coventry University, and a Bachelor of Arts in Person-Centred Counselling and Psychotherapy from the University of Warwick.

Laura also identifies as a Wounded Healer and describes the Sacred Wounding of her childhood and young adulthood as pivotal to the work she does in the world today. Without it, she would not feel driven to help and support others to (re)connect with their authentic sexuality and to free themselves from lives that are too small and constricted. Laura believes we can awaken at any time in our lives—no matter our background and experiences—and she especially champions older women not to let age hold them back from their truth and power. When not online or on retreat, Laura can be found in nature, especially in the woods where, as a dendrophile, she finds healing, guidance, connection and joy.

www.drlauramonk.com

Chapter 17

The Bracelet & The Seed

Anne Garland

"Margaret, you can get dressed now, and I will see you in my office," said Doctor van Buren.

While getting dressed, Margaret mumbled to herself *how are we going to afford another mouth to feed? We can't even keep up with feeding and caring for the riding school horses. And the kids? All four need new clothes and shoes. We are stretched so thin now and Ken is working all day and then works hours for the school. So how are we going to manage another child? Richie is almost four, and I thought I was done having kids. Although I do hope it's a girl this time. Nancy would be a wonderful big sister. Four boys would be a handful for sure.*

Margaret was lost in her thoughts when the nurse, Doctor van Buren's wife, interrupted.

"The doctor is waiting," she said.

Margaret hurried into his office and sat in the uncomfortable wooden straight-back chair across from the desk. Doctor van Buren, with his head down, looked up over his glasses.

"You have a tumor, Margaret, and we should operate as soon as possible for health reasons." Shocked at this unexpected news, Margaret replied, "Tumor?! I thought I was pregnant! I've missed my period for three months. I think it's been three months. Are you sure?"

Doctor van Buren, a long-time friend of her family, shook his head. "Yes, I'm sorry, Margaret. I'm sure. Go home, rest and we will make arrangements to take care of this as soon as possible."

Margaret left the office and greeted her husband, Ken, in the waiting room. Margaret conveys the news to him that they are not pregnant and what the doctor said about her condition.

"A tumor? You have been throwing up for weeks," Ken says. "I was hoping for a girl."

They drove home in silence as tears slowly rolled down Margaret's cheeks.

Two weeks passed. Margaret lay in their bed late at night thinking about the impending tumor surgery when that all-too familiar flutter crossed over her belly, the same flutter she felt countless times with each of her four pregnancies. She abruptly sat up and nudged Ken awake. "It's not a tumor! We are pregnant," she smiled. "I just felt the baby kick. I knew I was pregnant."

Richie turned four that July, and Anne (that's me!) was born two months later in early September.

The Bracelet

Life on the family farm was quickly becoming financially more draining on my parents. And, boarding and feeding the horses at the riding school was growing more time consuming and far more expensive than my family could bear. We were going bankrupt. Margaret, my mom, got a job and returned to working in real estate. Ken, my dad, continued working his blue-collar job while also doing side gigs plumbing. It wasn't enough to get by.

We eventually left the farm. I was three when we moved into a two-family home also referred to as a "flat" until we could get back on our feet—with seven of us tightly crammed in. We endured three more moves in four years. Then, on year five, we settled in our final family home on the lake just south of Saratoga, NY. It was perfect for us kids. The property had a dock with both short and tall diving boards, a boathouse, and even a cabana for changing into our bathing suits. With four acres to roam, the yard boasted less acreage than the farm—but it was kid heaven! And we always had plenty of kids, family, and friends to share in our oasis.

Many days the boys and their friends would swim to the docks across the lake. It was a distance and a good challenge. They would catch their breath before returning back. The Fannings, a childless couple who owned the dock where they usually landed, greeted my brothers happily and became quite fond of them, especially Kenny. Kenny reminded them of their only son who was killed in the Korean War in 1953. The Fannings owned the small village market. It wasn't long before the boys would ride their bikes to help out doing odd jobs at the market, in addition to their paper routes. They would often row the boat over to their dock and spend a lot of time at the Fanning home eating lunch or dinner or playing cards and games together. It was a relief that the younger boys were well supervised while our mom and dad continued to work and my two eldest siblings went off to college.

The Fannings became an important part of my brothers' lives growing up. They became their beacon of stability and trust to guide them toward a better future.

Very generous, the Fannings invited us to visit every Christmas. Mrs. Fanning served cookies and hot chocolate and presented gifts to all three of us. Not just one or two gifts, she would shower us with multiple surprises. It felt like we had two Christmases. One year stands out among the rest. I remember very clearly one special gift she gave me. I must have been 10. It was a small box, beautifully wrapped like all the others. I unwrapped it ever so carefully to find a beautiful white velvet box inside. When I lifted the spring-top lid and peered inside, the light above my head reflected on the gold of the bracelet inside the box before me. I marveled at the most beautiful gold bracelet I had ever seen. Releasing it carefully from the hooks holding it in place, I dangled it and admired its gold charm. One side was solid smooth gold, and the other side was a small glass bubble that encased some sort of yellow seed. As I looked up quizzically to Mrs. Fanning, she smiled.

"It's a mustard seed, dear," she said to me.

As I looked at the magnificence of the gold bracelet and shiny charm dangling from my delicate hands, I didn't need to say a word. Mrs. Fanning read the pure delight and gratitude in my face.

"A mustard seed is mentioned several times throughout the Bible as a symbol of faith," she said. "If you have faith as small as a mustard seed, nothing shall be impossible for you. It is also known to signify good luck."

Smiling back at Mrs. Fanning, I felt an unexplained wave of warmth throughout my body. I reached out to her and gave her the biggest embracing hug.

"Thank you," I wept. I knew as long as I owned this

bracelet luck would always be with me.

Faith & The Networker

Growing up our family was not particularly religious in practice. But, from that Christmas forward—the Christmas when I received the mustard seed, I embraced the word "faith." It was now forever planted in my soul. I somehow knew that I would be safe no matter what. That's not to say life was easy. Many life lessons appeared on the road in front of me.

At 17, and a senior in high school, I watched as my classmates planned college tours and career searches. My reality was choosing the path of a working girl and skipping the college route until later. Eventually, I did return to college, but at the time, I did not want to incur financial debt. Watching my parents struggle taught me what I didn't want to do. I kept the faith that some opportunity would come along, and it did.

I secured a job at the local telephone company in Schenectady, NY, as a long-distance telephone operator where they offered me a work-training program. The telephone company only offered this opportunity to a select few senior graduates who chose not to pursue college. I interviewed, tested, and started in January of my senior year and committed to full-time upon graduation in June. Making a living and a life for myself where I could be totally independent mattered to me.

Within six months I was promoted to their customer service team where I was introduced to sales. That sales job set the trajectory of my career networking with people in sales.

Listening and connecting, I quickly proved I was a people person. Networking came naturally to me, especially after I left the phone company and into corporate sales positions selling on the road. Somehow, I always knew someone somewhere who needed to be connected to another person so that they both could grow.

Not long after settling into my corporate sales roles, I became the "go to girl" whenever someone wanted to meet someone.

Faith & Timing

There is something fundamental about the seven-year itch in life—when one feels a sense of stagnation, usually in a marriage or relationship. For me, it was seven years since my divorce after a 21-year marriage to my children's father and two short term relationships. What filled my soul most when I wasn't traveling was creating and leading various events bringing women together to inspire and support each other. Our circle was growing bigger and so were my events.

Then, the universe gifted me Keith, "The One." We knew right away, and within a year, we married. I got my dream wedding.

Upon returning to Boston from our romantic European honeymoon, snuggled in the backseat of the limo at the airport, my cell phone rings. It was an HR manager calling. She was from a new company that recently acquired BASF, a Fortune 100 company where I was working the ideal corporate job of my lifetime—in their textile division. This job allowed me to excel at creating and hosting extraordinary experiential events for some of the top architects and designers in the Northeast. As the regional manager with a beautiful office on NYC's Fifth Avenue, I was known for my "not to miss events." After 9/11, my regional office relocated to Old Saybrook, CT.

I loved my job, and now the HR manager I didn't even know told me, "While your resume is impressive, we do not have a position for you, or quite frankly, the other three regional managers." She advised me to take the retirement package.

Stunned, I turned to Keith, my new husband.

"I'm losing my job," I said. He reassured me it would be fine.

Life is constantly changing, and we adapt. Thank you, Faith.

Isn't it funny, while one door opens, another door closes? This is where Faith walks in again. She is always by my side.

I had six months of severance to figure out my next move, which was short-lived

In less than six months, I was back on the road in the corporate world sporting a national position for a start-up. I always love a challenge!

Happily married and reinvented professionally, I still missed my gal pals. So, I continued this side gig gathering them together.

Often, on a more serious side, I was also someone whose street smarts, heart, and solid corporate sales background helped me to become a life advisor to many.

After three years and two more mergers and acquisitions, I hung up my corporate life for good. Hello again, Faith!

Feeling the energy to go all-in, I attended a women's event in NYC in 2008 that I saw advertised in a well-known women's magazine. The event's production, quality of speakers blew me away. Immediately, I decided that Connecticut women needed to experience this too. That's when Anne Garland Enterprises, LLC was born.

I collaborated with a wonderful woman and a like minded event planner. For me it was a labor of love and ten months of planning we birthed The Idea Circle for Women Conference, October 2009.

In addition to opening, lunch, and closing keynotes, we hosted 12 workshops, 30 speakers, honored a Woman of the Year and chose a non-profit for giving back to the community. The energy and excitement grew. Women wanted more, and I wanted to keep serving.

When my event partner moved on, I ran this program solo for four more years, changing lives and giving women a stage, a voice, and confidence. I could see changes and growth in women that only fueled me more...until it didn't.

I burned out after my fifth year.

That January in 2014 I chose to have foot surgery with six weeks of recovery to slow me down. Not knowing what was next, I learned to be still.

Today, eWN Greater Hartford exists because soon, like clockwork, someone reached out to recruit me for a growing national organization, eWomenNetwork. She wanted me to start a chapter in Connecticut.

At the time, only 25 chapters scattered across the states

with no representation in the Northeast. Granted, a few tried; they all failed. The closest chapter was central New Jersey. Reluctantly I said, "Yes." The stars aligned, and I made history leading eWomen Network's fastest-growing chapter in history becoming Executive Managing Director in 9 months with 100 new members. I was elected to their Advisory Board of 5. We were instrumental in scripting eWN's value statements.

High achieving women with heart sought connection and fun with an opportunity to lift others as they lifted themselves. I was a catalyst for their change and growth. Today I thank and applaud Aina Hoskins for her masterful leadership in continuing my legacy as Executive Managing Director.

One of my favorite eWN offerings that I hosted is their Strategic Business masterminds, aka, SBI's, where we gather 8-12 women to take a deep dive into a challenge each faced and, collectively, help create solutions. It changed the lives for many, giving clarity, confidence, and strength where before some saw little hope for their personal and professional situations.

During one morning SBI, a young woman so poised, sophisticated, and well put together spoke eloquently. She was clearly intelligent yet reserved. Something exceptional about her jumped out. I reached out to her afterward as I did so often as a networker. But this exchange was different. I wanted her to join the chapter, yet she had no money at the time. Fleeing from a bad relationship, and barely surviving herself while caring for her young daughter, she borrowed money from her daughter's piggy bank for gas to come to the meeting.

I took her under my wing and mentored her until she gained the strength to fly and eventually soar. She found her voice again after losing it through emotional abuse. Eventually, she became an integral leader on our chapter board. Today she is using her many business and sales skills as president of another women's group out of the state and mentoring entrepreneurs nationally. Thankfully, we both can look back now and laugh that she was a mess in a dress when I met her, and today she is a rising success.

This story is only one of the hundreds of women I have helped to find their voice and go from the sidelines to the spotlight. My life lights me up. I get to shine my light on others, embody Faith, give hope and possibilities when many see none.

Faith & Growth

At the end of 2019, while identifying my own goals for 2020, I decided it was time for me to step up my game with a new focus. Knowing so many women with big messages that the world needs to hear, I wanted to give them access to bigger public speaking stages. I knew I needed to travel that road of growth first in order to more effectively lead the way.

I called upon Faith again, took a leap, and signed up as an Aspiring Speaker of the National Speakers Association (NSA), Connecticut chapter. I attended my first meeting in January 2020 and received a warm reception from several Board members. Within two weeks, I was recruited to be president and bring my expertise in leadership, membership expansion, and event planning to help grow the chapter.

I was on a fast course to becoming a Professional Member of the National NSA, the precursor to being President-Elect, then President of the chapter to serve on their Board. This time I would be serving both men and women in the business of speaking. I helped several others become Professional members and tapped them to serve on the Board, giving each the visibility and confidence to serve others and speak on bigger stages.

Then, COVID hit. Everything changed. Everyone needed to adapt. We navigated the worst, held on, and remained focused on our goals.

And it was Faith that carried us through and made us stronger as a team and community.

Faith, Fun, Hope & Trust

As the days have turned into years and years have turned into decades, I still cherish the bracelet that Mrs. Fanning gifted me. To this day, it holds a special place in my jewelry box and reminds me of the deep-rooted faith she planted in my soul on that special Christmas morning. Mrs. Fanning gave me the gift of faith and possibility.

It's a wonder how such a small seed can grow to become a large tree. But, that's the meaning behind the inspiration for the mustard seed. "If you have faith as small as a mustard seed, nothing shall be impossible for you."

Immersed in a man's world of sales for decades, I learned to gather ladies together for "Girls' Night Out"—a lot. Letting loose and connecting with other women was—and still is—really important for balance and fun.

I've often been told that I possess a certain something that sets me apart. Someone described my faith in others as "an extraordinary ability to nudge" people "into their futures like a baby bird being volunteered to fly for the first time."

Apparently, I know others "can fly even if they don't yet!"

I love that I see doors opening and possibilities abounding for others where they might see only doubt.

To everyone, I say...

Keep the faith, be courageous, be vulnerable. Remember, "What the mind can conceive, the mind can achieve."

Some people believe "faith" and "hope" mean the same thing.

To me, "faith" is an end-goal, and hope?

"Hope" is a true desire and a dream. We hope something will take place but hope is not so deep a belief as faith.

Faith is the belief, or a knowing, that something is going to happen, and that all our hopes will come to fruition.

Faith allows us to create our goals. Goals are dreams in action.

Start with a dream, set a goal, then build a plan – and that will bring us closer to our goal.

Dreamers only fail when their desire and faith in following through falter.

We must have faith in ourselves that we can reach any goal; and we will as long as our desire is strong enough. Just trust.

The Gift

Hope is what we pass along from one person to another.

I now want to pass it on to you. Please contact me through email listed at the end of this chapter and request "The Seed." Then, I will send you your own seed charm of hope as my gift to you.

"If you have faith as small as a mustard seed, nothing shall be impossible for you."

God Bless

Anne Garland

About Anne

You've heard of six degrees of separation? Well, Anne Garland can cut that down to one. Anne (pronounced Annie) is the ultimate connector—and has literally been so since her early career starting with the telephone company. And in a world where who you know can be more powerful than what you know—Anne knows how to bring the right people together and produce bold, positive results.

Anne taps into a vast resume that includes working for top international brands like BASF, Honeywell, Hanes Knitwear, Applied Textiles, and others. Her keen marketing and sales skills, coupled with her interior design creativeness she honed with Kagan Architects, Connecticut delivers a one-two combination of punches that knocks out the competition by bringing the best out of people and teams.

As an award-winning presenter and event producer, Anne makes it her mission to inspire others. Passionate about empowering women entrepreneurs, her goal is to motivate women from playing roles behind the scenes to taking center stage. Anne's solo book, *Secrets of a Serial Worker* is to be released in late fall 2021. She is also a contributing author of *Make Your Connections Count: The Art of Connecting People,* Thrive Publishing. No matter what your professional need is, Anne has your back with a vision to put you on center stage.

Anne lives between her two homes, fifty semi-wooded acres in rural Connecticut and the summer beach house in Old Lyme enjoying the best of both diverse worlds with her husband Keith and their two beautiful collies. She also loves riding their motorcycle through the back roads viewing the

Connecticut you never really see when in a car. And she enjoys the time she spends with her grandchildren.

www.AnneGarlandEnterprises.com

LinkedIn @ Ann(i)eGarland

IG @ AnneGarlandEnterprises

FB @ eventsbyAnneGarlandEnterprises

Chapter 18

Being a Light

Debbie Sodergren

My purpose is to be a light. "What *does* that mean, you ask?" Great question, I get that all the time.

For me, being a light means showing up as a spiritual guide for other humans. As spiritual beings having a human experience, we tend to only show parts of ourselves, depending on the situation.

When I was four years old, I had to have open heart surgery twice. Everyone is born with a hole in their heart and it usually closes up on it's own by the age of four. While getting my kindergarten physical, my doctor noticed that my hole had not closed up. I was seen by a specialist who recommended I have open heart surgery. After my first surgery, my parents came into my room to see me. My mom noticed that my color was "funny" and said so to the nurse. My parents were asked to step outside my room while I was examined. While sitting outside my room waiting to see me, staff members were bringing in units of blood for me because I was bleeding out internally. The surgeon spoke to my parents and explained that the stitches he put in were not holding the tissue together. Apparently, while I was being moved from the surgery table to a gurney, the stitches tore and I would now need a second surgery. This is a lot for a four year old to go through, already after an eight-hour surgery, to need to go through it again and frankly, my parents were worried.

I believe that it was during my second open heart surgery that I experienced my out of body experience. I remember it, however, when I explain it, it filters through my four year old self. I remember floating above my body and slowly looking down at the body of 'her' on the table and the doctor and nurses around her. I remember this spaghetti string of light going from my belly button to hers. I remember turning back upward and continuing to go up, up, up. It was bright with light, like standing at night in front of a car with it's headlights on. I would feel these soap bubbles pass by me and when we connected, it was like I knew everything there was to know about that soap bubble as if they were a person. I felt happy, a giddy-happy. I was not afraid. I felt warm, comfortably warm. I felt loved and safe and so connected to everything around me. I remember realizing that I needed to go back to 'her' because I had a family and friends that I wanted to be with again. I felt I would return to this place someday and I wasn't sad to leave it.

I healed amazingly and have never had any issues.

After returning home from my surgery, I had these vivid 'dreams' of leaving my body and visiting my grandparents across the street in their house or my best friend next door. I didn't think much of it and thought everyone could do it. This experience was exciting to me. I shared it with adult family members who told me not to talk about it and if I did, people would think I was crazy. So, I didn't talk about it. Ever. I squashed it deep deep down inside because I didn't want to be different, weird, called a liar or be laughed at. I thought that because adults didn't want me to talk about it that it was a bad thing. Now that I am an adult, what I know is that they were full of fear about it because they did not understand.

It took a lot of therapy and curiosity and courage for me to revisit this part of my life and integrate it into my whole expression of who I am and what my purpose is. Being a light.

It happened when I decided to go back to college and I was taking a psychology course and the instructor told us about other courses she teaches about parapsychology. I wanted to learn more about what that was and inquired after class. When the instructor told me what parapsychology was, I had goosebumps so big all over my body and my being/soul was screaming *Yes! Yes! You found it! This is your journey!* It felt like I was revisiting information that I already knew inside of me. During those six years of school, one of the courses I was introduced to was the study of death and dying where we wrote our own obituary and studied Elizabeth Kubler Ross's work. This made death normal for me and not something to be afraid of.

Another course I loved was on channeling. This course re-connected me to my ability to communicate with others who have died, and angels, guides and even other beings from the far reaches of our galaxy. It wasn't until 2016 that I shared this knowledge.

I mastered being all of my essence and that gave me courage to go out into the world and share my light. You see, in the experience of my surroundings and growing up, I realized that I built beliefs about death that didn't fit me but I didn't have the knowledge or words to express why they didn't fit me. Lack of knowledge keeps us in fear. Fears that we witness in the adults we are surrounded with when we were young and impressionable, we took on as our own fear. When I had that ah-ha moment, I started to look at other parts of my life where I was being afraid and by facing those fears, I was able to be a light for others who wanted to know more of what I knew.

This led me to building a business where I help others who are frustrated, looking for answers about what is the meaning of life and how they can create their happiness, right now! By sharing strategies and tools that helped me, I can now shine a light and be of service to others. The only constant is change, which is transformation.

When someone decides to see me for energy work, I feel so honored. That means that I will have an opportunity to shepherd them on a part of their life journey. I consider this such an honor. This is delicate, sensitive and a huge step in trust. I get it because I too had to start there. It's not as scary as it seems. I have many options to meet people where they are at. If they want to do it on their own, they can read my book, *Just Be: Your Path to Meditation and Awareness,* by DJM Sodergren. If they want more, I offer a self study course on mindfulness meditation and one centered around figuring out what your beliefs are. For those who want accountability and access to me and messages from the other side, they can work with me one-on-one. When someone hires me to work with them one-on-one, we start by filling out a questionnaire so I have a better understanding of what the struggle is, and what the solution is they are looking for. From there, we see each other either in person or online for sessions. Most clients go out and practice what they have learned and return months later to do the next layer of the process.

Stepping into the spotlight of figuring out who you are and how your experiences shape you, is not for the faint of heart. It takes courage, lots of it. It takes trust in someone who you identify with that you trust. If you choose to do the work of really looking at what this life is all about, you will attract your mentor. It's how it works. That is one of the seven Laws of Attraction, but that is a whole other chapter!

About Debbie

Debbie Sodergren is an Energy Body Vibration Expert, Founder and CEO of Up Vibrations, LLC, best-selling author and international speaker. Debbie graduated from the New England School of Metaphysics in 1998. She is nationally certified as a Reiki Master Teacher, certified to teach Metaphysics and Meditation and an Infinite Possibilities Trainer Trailblazer. Debbie has been trained with knowledge in the human energy field in areas of chakra balancing, vibrational medicine, channeling, death and dying, meditation, astrology and mindset work of infinite possibilities.... just to name a few. Debbie has a deep understanding of the body, mind and spirit connection and knows that we are all connected, and as a business owner, this affects your business. Debbie has worked for over 20 years with many awakened and conscious women (and a few brave men) who are up to unapologetically living life all in. They take big risks and sometimes, get to the edge and need someone to reel them back in from the stress and overwhelm which effs up the other areas of their lives. She has taught in a classroom setting, offers energy work sessions and has one-on-one private sessions servicing clients in personal and business by getting Clarity and Strategies to make the big shifts as they live their purpose-filled lives.

www.debbiesodergren.com

Chapter 19

Amplify the Light

Dr. Davia H. Shepherd

I'm sitting down to write and it is close to the end of the day. I've had a long productive day in the office filled with things I love such as seeing patients who fill me with joy and laughter. I met with staff who made me feel well-supported. I also did some work for my women's group Ladies' Power Lunch (LPL). All in all, a fulfilling and wonderful day with so much that lends itself to gratitude.

And yet as I sit here I do not feel energized by an amazing day, but tired; a bone-level, soul-crushing exhaustion. I'm feeling this way because, dear friend, I have a secret.

Many of us have come to the thing we do as our work from the desire to support ourselves and our families but also from the place of wanting to be of service to the greater good. It's like a siren's call that we were probably exposed to at an early age. A deep desire to be helpful and to be of service. No matter what direction you went in, if it was providing hair care services, being an attorney or a coach, whatever was fun for you and made your heart glad, there was still the underpinning of wanting to be of service.

That's what it means to BE The BEACON. It means that you use the unique talents that make you yourself. The thing that you find fun, that you could do all day long. Take that thing and make a comfortable, abundant, supportive living doing it! And, while you are at it, share the light you shine with those in your world to help them shine *their* light, so they can help others shine *their* light in an infinite interwoven web of brilliance that eventually lights the entire world, to advancement, alignment, and enlightenment.

Usually when I tell stories, it's from my healed places. But the story I share today is one I'm deep in right now. I can share it with confidence however because I am able to look out towards the other side. You know that feeling when you see the light at the end of the tunnel? That's where I am. What I know for sure, having lived enough of life, is that the thing that we struggle with puts us in a unique position to help others on that path with the same microcosm of issues.

My deep secret is that I've been so defined by my profession that I could not see what was lighting me up. I could not see where my innate talents really lie and I couldn't access the most precious gift that I have to share with the world. As a result of that, I have not been truly living my passion.

All my adult life I have been on some sort of personal development/ self improvement kick. One of my mentors likes to joke that she spent 10 years in the personal development aisle. My comeback has always been: *I've got you beat, I've been in the personal development aisle since I was a teenager!*

It was therefore no accident that even though my background was focused in science and research, I fell in with the spiritual entrepreneur crowd once I started my own small business. The catalysts for my personal transformation included the type of business coaches I chose as I learned more about growing a business, and the entrepreneurs that I chose to get close to as I networked and got to know other small business owners.

Growing up I always got the hidden, or not so hidden messages that I was too much. Too much of a *"Know- the- more-est,"* I had too many big ideas, I talked too much about things kids had no business talking about. So I learned to be quiet and introverted. I learned to keep my big ideas to myself even though they were rarely if ever wrong, and I learned to hide my light.

I remember back when our LPL networking group was new, perhaps eight years ago. I had an opportunity to meet and talk to many entrepreneurs and small business owners about the nuts and bolts of their businesses. It was interesting that I started noticing that after every meeting, there would be at least one person who would lag behind to "pick my brain about her business." I'm a sharer and so once asked, answers would pour right out. We would see each other the following month or sometimes they would reach out before the month had ended. What was consistent was that they always had a positive experience to share about what happened when they implemented a suggestion of mine or what happened when they built on a thought that I shared that sparked something else for them.

I remember chatting with my friend Chloe White about this phenomenon. I'm a recovering researcher, after all. I was collecting the anecdotal evidence. I mentioned to her that when people come to me with tricky questions about their businesses, it was almost as though I could see a flowchart in my head about what their next steps should be to achieve the growth they desired. This struck me as odd. I could see their business trajectory so clearly, even though I had never been to business school, I prided myself on always having a business coach, and because I could never turn this "talent" around to work on my own business. Without fail however, this "talent" would show up for other people's businesses in a way that almost felt like a divine download. Chloe has always been a fountain of great advice for me and I remember her saying to me, "Maybe you should become a coach."

"What? Me, be a coach? I'm a physician! I don't have those types of credentials. I need to stay in my lane!" Those were just a few of the excuses that I came up with to hide the part of me that wanted to shine forth and support our community in this specific way. Tapes played in my mind of being a little girl and being dismissed as not knowing about things that I wasn't trained to know, but somehow had the information in my head. I tucked that weirdness away and played it safe. I stopped sharing with so many of our members and would only share with a very select few and my episodes of sharing became fewer and farther between.

Here I am eight years later. Through learned experience, coaching, certifications, learning about my human design and honing the "talent" with a few of my select and closest friends and mentors, I now have a handle on what it is that has been trying to come through me all these years since I was a child.

I have learned that I am an AMPLIFIER. A–what–now? Yep, you heard right, I am an amplifier. It has been explained to me in two ways by my mentors. The explanation that feels a little easier for me to stomach as a recovering researcher is that I'm just sharing my learned and lived experience and I have a tremendous capacity for "in the moment recall."

I know there is some truth to that. I've worked for major corporations for over a decade and then I've been in my own business for 11 years. I've learned a lot through my coaches and mentors and I've done certifications. There is a lot of knowledge rattling around in this skull of mine. That being said, I can feel the truth of the deeper explanation as easily as I feel sunshine on a sunny day.

The deeper explanation goes a little something like this: If you believe that everything is energy, then you will understand that there is some energetic exchange that takes place when we are in each other's energy fields. What I now understand is that when you step into my energy field, my energetic field acts sort of as a projection screen for yours. In that moment if I can let go of EGO, let go of how weird this all is, and also let go of any "have-to's," then without fail, beautiful wisdom flows through. Often I do not recognize what comes through as coming from my mind per say but how I would describe it is: I reflect back and put voice to what your energy is communicating. I can put your energy into words. And not only do I translate your energy into language, but your ideas become the biggest and best form of themselves in my space.

Sometimes when I begin sharing, "This is what I see for you..." and launch into what may seem like a traditional business strategic plan, the ideas make no sense to me personally. I will often ask, "Is this resonating for you?" When I ask this question I see the answering light of recognition in their eyes. The relief that comes from being seen and understood and I know then that I am on the right track. That is the work of an amplifier.

That would explain why I had such a deep sense of knowing as a child of things that no child, or not many children at any rate, would have any knowledge of. It was just a reflection of the energy that I was immersed in, in the moment. And as you can imagine, that was not well received and has been my secret shame and one of the things I've kept hidden about myself for decades.

Why am I sharing this story with you here and now? What does it have to do with being the beacon? If you got attracted to a book called *Be the Beacon*, chances are that you resonate with the idea that shining our light is not only a good thing to do, but that it is essential. You probably look at your vocation as more than just a paycheck and more of a calling. You probably totally recognize that if we lived in a world where we were all shining our beautiful lights and being the heart-centered leaders we are called to be, we would create a more loving and kind life for generations to come. But many of us are going about our beacon-ness half-assed instead of full-assed.

What are the parts of you that would be tremendously supportive of your business, your passion, your calling, your beacon? What are the parts of you that you keep hidden because perhaps as a child you too may have been encouraged to hold back, be less, be not too much? You fill in the blank here. Could letting that part of you out to breathe be just what you and your business need to shine your light most radiantly?

What would be available to you in life and in your business if you weren't expending energy managing your reputation?

What if you just trusted life completely, thwarted convention, worried less about being socially acceptable and instead allowed your gifts to shine through you?

Would that version of you be the version that saw more of the small miracles and coincidences that make life richer?

Would that make your life fuller, richer and more lived in?

It might seem like a lot to ask but the results are detrimental if we don't head in this direction.

There is a quote that I like. I wish I could give it attribution but every time I see it, it is listed as anonymous or unknown:

"A downed lighthouse is more dangerous than a rocky reef."

When did the idea that we are all here for a reason, a soul purpose, become a radical idea? I've had this conversation with patients in the treatment room, and while I find that most people politely agree with me when I postulate the idea that we are all geniuses, I can see the wheels in their minds working, suggesting, *"This doc is a super weirdo. Good thing she is helping my pain, because her ideas are way out there."*

Imagine a world where you don't have to hide the essence of what makes you yourself, and where that actually supports you to live your optimal life. Where you know that you are not broken and you have absolute permission to just be yourself.

When you as a beacon demonstrate life in a better way, other beacons learn from your example. You embracing your gifts actually gives others permission to be in their gifting as well and then we work together in the divine harmony that is intended, each of us working in the area that lights us up and brings us joy. And a world with more joy? Well, what could be better than that?

This is the principle upon which our Ladies Power Lunch Community is built. It is a group of women and a few men in business who embrace the idea of being themselves in their truest expression, both in their lives and in their businesses and who intentionally and in an aligned way support each other and each other's businesses to foster business growth and personal development. Doesn't it just sound like a heavenly place? It is. It is free and you are invited to play.

About Davia

Dr. Davia H. Shepherd is a holistic physician and master connector. A certified retreat leader and recovering researcher, she is celebrating almost 20 years in various areas of healthcare. She loves public speaking and is an international speaker and bestselling author. She helps female entrepreneurs live the best version of their lives in every area: health, business, relationships, finances. She leads transformational retreats, conferences, and Ladies' Power Lunch networking events. Davia lives in the suburbs in Connecticut with her outstanding husband, Wayne, two amazing miracle boys, Preston and Christian, and her mom, Phyllis.

www.ladiespowerlunch.com

Chapter 20

Shining Your Light

Elizabeth B. Hill, MSW

Birthing an anthology is not for the faint of heart. As I met with the authors and read their chapters, there were intense waves of energy to ride. Sometimes, life feels so magical and loving that I feel like my head and heart are just going to explode. As I read these stories of love-in-action, courage, healing, and divine intervention, I felt a kinship. I felt like I could relax with them. I felt like they got it. That they knew what it's like to choose to own our light. That these women will *encourage* me to shine my light, they will actually *get excited* when I shine bright. That they knew how scary this can be sometimes. And that this is a group of women who know how important it can be to shine a light for others that can't find their own light at the moment.

I feel so honored and blessed to have gotten to know these beautiful souls. Some I knew before we set to write our pages. Some I am just getting the gift of knowing. I have got to know them deeply through talking with them and reading their stories.

You may have felt drawn to one of the authors. Perhaps their story has remnants of your own. I invite you to reach out to any of the dear women who are courageous enough to share their stories and inspiration here. If you are drawn to them, there is a reason. I invite you to investigate!

I invite you to come play with us in Ladies' Power Lunch.

It is where I learned that I didn't have to sacrifice myself or who I was to be successful in business. It was where I learned not to hide my light under a bushel. It was where my business has flourished—and also where I have met some of my dearest friends.

I invite you to shine your light. This is a safe space to be you. We're here to tend your flame.

Love & Courage,

Elizabeth

Acknowledgements

Tremendous gratitude to all our BEACON authors, all our LPL members, staff, supporters, affiliates, and volunteers who continue to believe in our mission to be the beacon for the beacons.

Thank you Audra Garling Mika for your assistance in guiding many of our authors through the challenging process of sharing their stories.

Thank you Jaime Williams for being the glue that keeps the Green Heart Living Press ship together.

Special thanks to Sandy Krajick, Ashlie Woods, Darla LeDoux, Barb Prichard, Veronica Wirth, Collective Sisters, Wayne, Chris and Pres.

Stay LIT dear ones!

About Green Heart Living

Green Heart Living's mission is to make the world a more loving and peaceful place, one person at a time. Green Heart Living Press publishes inspirational books and stories of transformation, making the world a more loving and peaceful place, one book at a time.

Whether you have an idea for an inspirational book and want support through the writing process—or your book is already written and you are looking for a publishing path—Green Heart Living can help you get your book out into the world.

You can meet Green Heart authors on the Green Heart Living YouTube channel and the Green Heart Living Podcast.

www.greenheartliving.com

Green Heart Living Press Publications

Redefining Masculinity: Visions for a New Way of Being

Your Daily Dose of PositiviDee

Grow Smarter: Collaboration Secrets to Transform Your Income and Impact

Transformation 2020

Transformation 2020 Companion Journal

The Great Pause: Blessings & Wisdom from COVID-19

The Great Pause Journal

Love Notes: Daily Wisdom for the Soul

Green Your Heart, Green Your World: Avoid Burnout, Save the World and Love Your Life

Made in the USA
Columbia, SC
02 November 2021

48233997R00127

RÈGLES POUR
FAIRE PARLER
VOTRE HOMME...
ET POUR LE COMPRENDRE QUAND IL NE PARLE PAS!

Catalogage avant publication de la Bibliothèque nationale du Canada

Markman, Ann

Règles pour faire parler votre homme – : et pour le comprendre quand il ne parle pas!

(Collection Psychologie)

ISBN 2-7640-0791-4

1. Différences entre sexes (Psychologie). 2. Relations entre hommes et femmes. 3. Communication interpersonnelle. 4. Femmes – Psychologie. 5. Hommes – Psychologie. I. Titre. II. Collection : Collection Psychologie (Éditions Quebecor).

BF692.2.M37 2003   155.3'3   C2003-941755-7

LES ÉDITIONS QUEBECOR
7, chemin Bates
Outremont (Québec)
H2V 4V7
Tél. : (514) 270-1746

© 2004, Les Éditions Quebecor
Bibliothèque nationale du Québec
Bibliothèque nationale du Canada

Éditeur : Jacques Simard
Coordonnateur de la production : Daniel Jasmin
Conception de la couverture : Bernard Langlois
Illustration de la couverture : Veer
Révision : François Petit
Infographie : Composition Monika, Québec

Nous reconnaissons l'aide financière du gouvernement du Canada par l'entremise du Programme d'Aide au Développement de l'Industrie de l'Édition pour nos activités d'édition.

Gouvernement du Québec – Programme de crédit d'impôt pour l'édition de livres – Gestion SODEC.

Imprimé au Canada

ANN MARKMAN

RÈGLES POUR

FAIRE PARLER
VOTRE HOMME...

ET POUR LE COMPRENDRE QUAND IL NE PARLE PAS !

LES ÉDITIONS
Quebecor
QUEBECOR MEDIA

Un gros merci
à tous les hommes de ma vie.

Les hommes et les femmes: deux mondes

Les hommes et les femmes sont égaux, certes, mais ô combien différents! Particulièrement en ce qui a trait à la communication. En effet, la communication entre l'homme et la femme est souvent difficile. L'homme ne s'exprime pas comme la femme le souhaite, et celle-ci se sent incomprise parce qu'elle ne se sent pas écoutée lorsqu'elle s'exprime.

Pourtant, les hommes parlent et écoutent autant que les femmes, à la différence qu'ils ne le font pas dans les mêmes circonstances ni pour les mêmes raisons. La femme s'exprime pour entrer en relation avec l'autre ou pour approfondir le lien, tandis que l'homme s'exprime plutôt pour donner de l'information ou en demander. Une fois que l'on a identifié cela clairement, il est facile de comprendre qu'ils aient du mal à se comprendre!

Pour l'homme, le langage a une fonction utilitaire ; pour la femme, il a une fonction émotive. L'action est la priorité de l'homme ; s'il a un problème, il ne va pas en parler mais le régler. La femme, elle, va en parler afin de trouver une solution pour ensuite le régler.

Bien des femmes se plaignent que leur homme ne leur parle pas, qu'il n'exprime pas ses émotions ; elles ont l'impression qu'elles ne peuvent compter pour lui. Devant le mutisme de son homme, la femme se sent donc incomprise et rejetée. Selon elle, l'homme garde le silence alors qu'il devrait lui parler et se confier à elle. La femme pense qu'elle n'intéresse pas son homme, qu'il ne veut pas l'écouter parce qu'il ne lui accorde aucune valeur, parce qu'il ne l'aime pas.

Mais tout cela n'a rien à voir avec la réalité puisqu'en ne disant rien, l'homme communique avec sa compagne. Différemment, certes, mais il communique tout de même.

Ainsi, l'homme ne communique pas comme une femme, mais il communique. Croire que l'homme fonctionne exactement comme une femme sur le plan de la communication serait une erreur.

Ignorer la différence entre les hommes et les femmes en ce qui concerne la communication, c'est nier la réalité. Votre homme n'est pas un égoïste ou un demeuré parce qu'il ne pense pas et ne communique pas comme vous. Il n'est pas fait comme vous, voilà tout. Il pense et communique comme un homme parce qu'il est un homme, tout comme vous pensez et communiquez comme une femme parce que vous êtes une femme. Accepter que votre homme est différent de ce point de vue, c'est déjà être sur la bonne voie pour le comprendre et, surtout, le faire parler.

L'homme ne peut changer du jour au lendemain. Vous l'avez choisi, acceptez-le donc tel qu'il est. Vous ne pourrez changer ses comportements et ses attitudes ; tout ce que vous pouvez faire, c'est l'amener à en ajouter à ceux qu'il a déjà.

Avec son homme, on doit commencer par de petits pas. Changer petit à petit votre comportement par rapport à lui changera petit à petit son comportement par rapport à vous. Et c'est par de petits changements qu'on obtient de grandes transformations.

Comme nous l'avons dit précédemment, les hommes parlent tout autant que les femmes, mais pas pour les mêmes raisons ni dans les mêmes circonstances. Les femmes doivent donc apprendre à décoder le langage de leur homme si elles veulent réussir à le faire parler et à être enfin écoutée.

Respecter certaines règles vous permettra d'obtenir ce que vous voulez de votre homme sans vous oublier, sans vous sacrifier ni vous faire souffrir.

Ces règles ne représentent aucun danger pour votre homme, et vous n'aurez pas à le brusquer, à le manipuler ni à lui faire subir une séance de dressage intensif. Après tout, c'est un homme que vous voulez, pas un chien savant.

Les exigences

Le psychologue Joe Tanenbaum, auteur du livre *Male and female realities: understanding the opposite sex*, a réalisé une étude portant sur les changements que les hommes et les femmes aimeraient apporter chez leur partenaire. Cette étude a démontré, entre autres, que les changements demandés par la femme correspondent assez exactement à ce que la femme possède comme caractéristiques, et vice versa. On peut en déduire qu'il est difficile d'accepter et de comprendre que notre partenaire soit différent de nous. On aimerait bien qu'il agisse, pense et communique comme nous. Ce serait tellement plus simple ! Mais peut-être aussi plus ennuyant...

Particulièrement pour les hommes, qui ont une capacité d'adaptation assez limitée en général, ayant beaucoup de difficulté à s'adapter à la façon de communiquer de leur partenaire et à la comprendre. Il n'est donc pas étonnant que tant de femmes prennent en charge la santé de leur couple. Et c'est l'une des choses que cet ouvrage vous aidera à mieux comprendre.

Selon les résultats de l'étude de Joe Tanenbaum, les douze principaux changements demandés au sexe opposé sont les suivants:

Les hommes voudraient que les femmes...	Les femmes voudraient que les hommes...
1. Parlent moins;	1. Parlent davantage;
2. Soient moins émotives;	2. Soient plus émotifs;
3. Se dépensent plus physiquement;	3. Se dépensent moins physiquement;
4. Soient moins romantiques;	4. Soient plus romantiques;
5. Fassent l'amour plus souvent;	5. Soient plus sensuels et moins génitaux;
6. S'occupent moins des «autres»;	6. S'occupent plus des autres;
7. Soient plus rationnelles;	7. Soient plus spontanés;
8. S'occupent plus de leur carrière;	8. S'occupent plus de leur famille;
9. Restent plus souvent à la maison;	9. Sortent plus souvent;
10. Soient moins sensibles;	10. Aient davantage de compassion pour les autres;
11. Soient plus ponctuelles;	11. Soient moins pressés;
12. Se préparent plus rapidement.	12. Se préoccupent plus de leur hygiène.

Sans s'en rendre compte, bien des gens sont beaucoup plus exigeants envers leur partenaire qu'envers eux-mêmes. Or, une personne ne peut exiger d'une autre qu'elle soit exactement comme elle, qu'elle fasse exactement les mêmes choses qu'elle et qu'elle ait exactement les mêmes réactions qu'elle dans les mêmes circonstances. Chaque individu est responsable de sa vie, et ce qui est bon et utile pour une personne peut être mauvais et inutile pour une autre.

Dans un couple, il est facile d'accuser l'autre de mauvaise foi, de ne pas l'écouter et de ne pas le comprendre si on refuse d'accepter qu'il est différent, qu'il ne pense pas comme nous et ne communique pas comme nous. Qu'un couple se porte bien ou pas n'est pas seulement une question de volonté, d'intelligence ou d'amour ; c'est avant tout une question de communication.

On doit donc accepter qu'il y ait des différences entre les hommes et les femmes plutôt que de tenter d'uniformiser les partenaires pour faire en sorte qu'ils deviennent semblables. Le couple se compose de deux personnes très différentes, qui ont chacune une vie, des valeurs, une façon de penser et une manière de communiquer qui leur sont propres. Et ce sont ces différences entre elles qui font que le couple est un couple.

Si vous apprenez à écouter, à comprendre et à respecter votre homme dans son mode de communication, vous obtiendrez plus d'un avantage. Non seulement vous comprendrez mieux votre homme, mais il vous comprendra mieux lui aussi. Il deviendra rapidement conscient de vos besoins, car vous saurez lui en faire part correctement. Pour cela, il suffit de suivre certaines règles.

Qu'aimeriez-vous que votre partenaire change dans son comportement?

————◦————

« Je voudrais qu'il soit plus à l'écoute. Une fois sur deux, quand je lui parle, il ne répond pas. J'ai plus de réactions de la part de mon chien... »

Anabelle, 26 ans

————◦————

« J'aimerais qu'il m'aide un peu plus dans la maison et qu'il pense à s'occuper des enfants sans que j'aie à le lui demander. On les a eus à deux, ces enfants-là. Pourquoi est-ce que j'ai l'impression que je suis toujours la seule à m'en occuper ? »

Fanny, 32 ans

————◦————

« J'aimerais qu'il m'écoute un peu plus au lieu de toujours me dire quoi faire et de quelle façon il pourrait régler les choses s'il était à ma place. J'ai vraiment l'impression qu'il me croit incapable de m'en occuper toute seule et de trouver moi-même des solutions à mes problèmes. »

Solange, 37 ans

————◦————

« Je voudrais qu'il ramasse ses affaires et qu'il arrête de me prendre pour sa bonne. Je voudrais qu'il s'occupe un peu plus de la maison. Je voudrais qu'on sorte plus souvent et qu'il arrête, le samedi, de faire passer son golf avant sa vie de famille. Je voudrais aussi qu'il arrête de me demander de faire l'amour quand il sait que je n'en ai pas envie. Qu'il me parle plus de son travail, etc. »

Christiane, 29 ans

————◦————

« Bonne question... En fait, mon conjoint pourrait s'occuper un peu plus de moi, des enfants et de la maison, mais je ne lui demande rien et je ne crois pas qu'il soit capable de le deviner. Je préfère m'organiser toute seule, pourvu qu'il soit là et que je le sente aussi amoureux qu'au début. »

Mariska, 41 ans

———— ‹○› ————

« Je voudrais qu'il m'invite à sortir un peu plus souvent, sans que j'aie à lui tordre le bras. Il me semble que ce n'est pas trop demander... »

Angela, 24 ans

———— ‹○› ————

Règle nº 1

L'homme réfléchit en silence

« *Le plus grand des défis, pour la femme, c'est de soutenir et de comprendre son mari quand il se mure dans le silence.* »

John Gray

Pour écouter, comprendre et s'exprimer, les femmes font appel aux deux hémisphères de leur cerveau, et les hommes, à un seul. Cela explique en partie pourquoi les hommes ne répondent pas tout de suite quand on leur pose une question. Les femmes peuvent penser, écouter et parler en même temps, tout comme elles peuvent à la fois lire, parler au téléphone, écouter une émission et surveiller un plat au four. Pour l'homme, faire plus d'une chose à la fois est très difficile. Il va plutôt se concentrer sur une tâche à la fois et la terminer avant de passer à la suivante. Et il ne peut faire autrement car il est comme cela. Cela n'excuse pas tous les comportements indésirables de votre homme, mais cela permet de mieux en comprendre plusieurs.

Si vous avez l'impression que votre homme ne fait rien, c'est peut-être parce qu'il est en train de réfléchir à ce qu'il va faire. En effet, l'homme peut être silencieux quand il ne trouve pas de réponse à une question, quand il doit trouver une solution à un problème, quand il est stressé, contrarié ou peiné, quand il veut mettre de l'ordre dans ses idées ou qu'il a besoin de refaire le plein d'énergie ou de se retrouver. Autrement dit, l'homme est souvent silencieux.

Quand ça va mal, la femme cherchera tout de suite à en parler à quelqu'un en qui elle a confiance, et la plupart du temps cette personne sera son homme. Quand ça va mal, l'homme voudra plutôt se taire et s'isoler pour réfléchir et trouver une solution à ses problèmes. Pour se faire du bien, l'homme s'isole. La femme, elle, parle. L'homme a besoin d'une raison pour parler, alors que la femme ne le fait que pour le plaisir. Cette différence est si marquée qu'on peut même se demander s'ils sont faits pour vivre ensemble...

Le mécanisme de la pensée de l'homme fonctionne comme ceci : quand vous lui posez une question, il ne répond pas parce qu'il réfléchit. Et comme il ne peut parler et réfléchir en même temps, il ne dit rien. Au contraire, la femme réfléchit et parle en même temps avec facilité, ce qui est presque impossible pour l'homme.

Lorsque vous demandez à votre homme ce qui se passe et qu'il vous répond que tout va bien, n'insistez pas : il est probablement en train de réfléchir. Il vous parlera quand il sera prêt à le faire, quand il aura mis de l'ordre dans son esprit et qu'il aura formulé sa réponse correctement de façon à pouvoir l'exprimer. Et lorsqu'il s'impatiente à votre endroit parce que vous insistez pour qu'il vous réponde, soyez certaine qu'il ne vous dira rien. L'homme a besoin de s'isoler dans le silence pour parvenir à vous parler. Il ne peut vous écouter, réfléchir et vous parler tout à la fois. Il n'a pas votre polyvalence. Et s'il agit ainsi, ce n'est pas par mauvaise foi ou parce qu'il trouve que ce que vous dites n'est pas important, mais tout simplement parce qu'il a besoin d'y penser un peu plus longtemps.

Avant de parler, l'homme cherche la meilleure réponse, et s'il n'a pas reçu toutes les informations nécessaires pour le faire, il préférera ne rien répondre du tout. Par son silence, l'homme dit à sa compagne qu'il réfléchit et ne sait pas encore quoi dire. Lorsqu'il réfléchit en silence, votre homme absorbe tout ce que vous venez de lui dire. Il élabore toutes les réponses ou toutes les solutions possibles, puis choisit la meilleure. Ensuite, il formule celle-ci correctement dans sa tête, et après – mais seulement après –, il l'exprime.

Lorsque survient un problème, l'homme cherche à être seul, et la femme, à en parler. Pour lui, il est vital de se réfugier dans le silence. Pour elle, ce silence envoie plutôt un message de manque de respect, de manque d'intérêt, voire de manque d'amour.

Quand l'homme se réfugie dans le silence, la femme craint rapidement le pire. Elle se dit qu'il lui parlerait s'il l'aimait, car c'est ce qu'elle ferait dans les mêmes circonstances. Mais votre homme n'est pas vous, il n'est pas une femme et il ne réagit pas du tout comme vous le feriez dans les mêmes circonstances. Pour diminuer son stress, la femme a besoin de parler alors que l'homme a plutôt besoin de s'isoler.

Même si votre homme est follement amoureux de vous, il peut ressentir le besoin de s'isoler et de se taire. Plus votre homme est capable de s'isoler et a besoin de paix, meilleures sont les chances qu'il revienne vers vous dans de bonnes dispositions pour vous parler.

Une fois la période de silence terminée, vous retrouverez votre homme tel qu'il était auparavant, puisque ces périodes de solitude n'apportent pas de grands changements : elles font partie de lui, elles sont dans sa nature. Il a besoin de ce silence pour être capable de s'exprimer. Sans ces périodes de réflexion, votre homme ne peut savoir quoi vous dire, et s'il n'a rien à dire, il ne vous dira rien.

Lorsqu'un homme est toujours collé à sa partenaire, il devient irritable, a des sautes d'humeur et est toujours sur la défensive. Il n'aime pas se sentir « attaché » de force à sa partenaire. Autrement dit, si vous ne voulez pas voir votre homme s'éloigner de vous, donnez-lui de la corde. Plus il se sentira libre de s'isoler en silence, plus il sera enclin à répondre à vos besoins.

L'homme a besoin de cet isolement pour être capable de communiquer avec sa partenaire, il doit faire de l'ordre dans ses idées avant de les exprimer. Si les femmes pensent à voix haute, les hommes pensent seuls et en silence. Lorsqu'une femme ne laisse pas son partenaire avoir ces moments de tranquillité, il finit par s'éloigner d'elle de plus en plus et par ne lui dire plus rien, car il se sent étouffé, ne pouvant pas s'isoler pour se ressourcer, faire le plein et mettre de l'ordre dans son esprit.

Votre homme n'a pas besoin, comme vous, de discuter des problèmes et des difficultés pour les résoudre, il n'a besoin que d'une seule chose pour y arriver : la paix.

Si vous voulez favoriser un climat d'intimité avec votre homme, laissez-le s'isoler en silence. Sans ces moments de paix, votre homme perd vite le besoin de vivre des moments d'intimité avec vous. S'il ne peut pas s'éloigner de vous pour se retrouver, votre homme se mettra à prendre ses distances par rapport à vous et évitera toute discussion. Il a *besoin* d'être seul en silence pour mieux revenir vers vous, pour retrouver le désir d'être avec vous et pour mieux répondre à vos attentes. Plus votre homme peut s'isoler, plus il reviendra vers vous.

Si vous voulez aider votre homme, laissez-le tranquille ; il n'a pas besoin de vous. S'il a besoin de vous, il saura vous le dire. En attendant, ne tentez pas d'aller au-devant de ses désirs et laissez-le plutôt réfléchir en silence, tout comme il vous laisse réfléchir à voix haute.

Lorsqu'un homme est contrarié, blessé ou irrité, il cesse de parler pour mettre de l'ordre dans ses idées. Il reste en silence et ne veut pas être dérangé. La femme ne doit pas interpréter cela comme un affront, qu'il ne se tait pas pour blesser sa compagne mais bien pour trouver quelque chose à lui répondre.

Donc, ne reprochez pas à votre homme de ne pas vous parler, de ne pas se confier à vous, ne le boudez pas et ne vous fâchez pas contre lui. Plus vous lui reprocherez son silence, plus il s'y réfugiera et évitera de se confier réellement. Pire, il pourrait se mettre à vous mentir pour avoir la paix.

Ne poursuivez pas votre homme pour le faire parler en le suivant partout où il va, en le surveillant quand il veut avoir la paix ou en niant son besoin de solitude pour lui tenir compagnie à tout prix.

Ne punissez pas votre homme de ses moments de silence par du chantage émotif ou sexuel, des bouderies, de l'indifférence, des reproches, etc. Si vous le punissez, votre homme risque de ne jamais se rapprocher de vous après un moment d'isolement. Car alors vous lui feriez sentir qu'il n'agit pas correctement et en conclurait que vous ne le trouvez pas digne de vous parler. Qui a dit que les hommes n'étaient pas sensibles ?

Rassurez-vous et, surtout, raisonnez-vous, votre homme ne se tait pas pour vous faire souffrir, pour vous faire enrager ou parce qu'il ne vous écoute pas ; votre homme se tait parce qu'il a besoin de se taire. Et ne craignez rien, il sortira de son silence à un moment ou à un autre pour revenir vers vous. Lorsque vous respectez son silence, votre homme se sent aimé. Il sent que vous avez confiance en lui et que vous le soutenez. Et quand votre homme sait que vous lui faites confiance, il peut déplacer des montagnes.

« Les hommes réclament le droit d'être libres alors que les femmes réclament le droit de se sentir offensées. Les hommes ont besoin d'espace alors que les femmes ont besoin de compréhension. »

John Gray

Votre homme ne fonctionne pas comme vous, et si vous ne voulez pas du silence de votre partenaire comme réponse à vos questions, adressez-vous à votre amie, à votre sœur ou à votre mère. Une femme saura vous donner ce que vous voulez maintenant, alors votre homme pourra le faire uniquement lorsque sa période de silence et de réflexion sera terminée. Il faut parfois être patiente, car cela peut être long.

Lorsque votre homme ne vous répond pas ou ne vous parle pas, comment interprétez-vous son silence ?

« Je pense qu'il ne m'écoute pas parce que mes histoires l'ennuient. Il ne s'intéresse pas à moi, il refuse de me comprendre. »

Anabelle, 26 ans

« Je pense qu'il n'a pas compris ou qu'il fait exprès parce qu'il ne veut pas faire quelque chose pour m'aider. Parfois, je me dis qu'il est peut-être juste sourd. »

Fanny, 32 ans

———————◄○►———————

« Quand mon conjoint ne me répond pas, j'ai vraiment l'impression qu'il me prend pour une conne. Quand il se tait, ça lui évite d'avoir à faire des choses dans la maison. Il préfère ne pas répondre parce qu'il sait que je vais me débrouiller toute seule. »

Solange, 37 ans

———————◄○►———————

« Quand mon conjoint ne me répond pas, je pense qu'il est en train de chercher le meilleur mensonge pour me faire plaisir. J'ai vraiment l'impression qu'il ne me fait pas confiance parce qu'il n'est pas capable de me répondre spontanément. »

Christiane, 29 ans

———————◄○►———————

« S'il ne me répond pas, je crois tout de suite que je ne lui ai pas posé la bonne question au bon moment. C'est moche, parce que quand je lui parle, j'ai toujours l'impression de le déranger. »

Mariska, 41 ans

———————◄○►———————

« Je pense qu'il a quelque chose à me cacher et je m'efforce de lui faire cracher le morceau. Mais ça ne marche pas toujours, car plus j'insiste, moins il parle. Pourtant, il devrait comprendre que c'est important pour moi. Mais non. Peut-être qu'il est juste un peu con. »

Angela, 24 ans

Règle n° 2

Soyez claire et concise

Pour obtenir des réponses claires de la part de votre conjoint, vous devez lui poser des questions claires, et si possible portant sur un seul sujet à la fois, puisque l'homme
ne peut pas réfléchir à deux sujets ou plus en même
temps. Il n'est pas aussi polyvalent que vous.

Comme l'homme n'exprime pas ses pensées pendant
qu'il réfléchit à ce qu'il va vous répondre, son silence peut
être interprété comme un manque d'écoute. Aussi, lorsqu'une femme passe de longues minutes à parler à son
homme de tout ce qui lui passe par la tête, il l'interrompt
parce qu'il ne peut la suivre. La femme voit ces interrup-
tions comme un manque d'écoute.

Plus vous parlez, moins il écoute, car il n'a pas le
temps de réfléchir à ce que vous lui dites. L'homme per-
cevra alors sa compagne comme une chialeuse parce qu'il

ne comprend pas le but de ce sermon qu'il trouve interminable. Il ne sait pas que le fait de lui parler de vos ennuis vous fait du bien, et si vous ne le lui dites pas, ne comptez pas sur lui pour le deviner. Il se demande où vous voulez en venir et pourquoi vous lui dites tout cela. Et plus vous donnez de détails, moins il comprend.

Les hommes ne sont pas aussi clairvoyants et sensibles à leur entourage que nous le sommes, nous les femmes. Beaucoup de choses leur passent sous le nez sans qu'ils aient la moindre idée de ce qui vient de se passer. L'homme a de la difficulté à se mettre à votre place parce qu'il est plus cérébral que vous. Vous êtes plus émotive, et il ne peut pas comprendre vos besoins parce qu'il n'a pas les mêmes. Pour lui, l'émotion exprime le reproche ou un problème, et si vous êtes trop émotive en lui parlant, il se sentira vite attaqué même s'il n'a rien à se reprocher.

Toute leur vie, les femmes ont appris à prendre soin de leur entourage. Elles ont vu leur mère et leur grand-mère le faire. L'homme n'a pas eu ce genre de modèle. Il ne peut donc pas ressentir les besoins de son entourage, et encore moins les combler.

Lorsque vous lui parlez, votre homme croit tout de suite que vous lui reprochez quelque chose ou que vous le tenez responsable du problème; il ne peut voir d'autres raisons puisqu'il ne connaît que ces deux-là, et si vous ne lui dites pas pourquoi vous voulez qu'il vous parle, il ne le saura jamais. Ne pensez pas que l'homme peut comprendre votre intention pendant que vous lui parlez;

toutes ses énergies sont utilisées à vous écouter et à recueillir l'information.

Si quelque chose vous préoccupe, parlez-lui-en clairement. Ne lui faites pas de reproches. Parlez-lui plutôt de vous, de vos sentiments, de ce que vous ressentez. Expliquez-lui en quoi cela vous préoccupe. Vous pourriez être surprise par sa grande sensibilité et par ses attentions délicates s'il a une idée claire de ce qui se passe dans votre tête. Sans cela, ne comptez pas sur lui pour le deviner.

Aussi, si vous voulez qu'il fasse quelque chose pour vous faire plaisir, dites-le-lui clairement. Sinon, il ne le devinera pas, car il n'est pas comme vous. Une des prochaines règles a trait à ce que vous devez lui dire pour l'amener à faire tout ce que vous voulez, ou presque.

Lorsque la femme souhaite que l'homme lui réponde autre chose que oui ou non, elle doit lui poser des questions qui peuvent avoir pour réponses autre chose que oui ou non. L'homme a besoin de questions précises pour être capable de donner une réponse précise. Si les questions posées sont vagues, évasives, l'homme ne donnera que des réponses vagues et évasives.

Assurez-vous également que vos questions sont courtes. Ne vous perdez pas dans un amas de détails, vous mêleriez votre homme. Quelques mots de plus et vous risquez de le perdre complètement! Allez directement au but: il y a plus de chances d'avoir une réponse à des questions courtes qu'à des questions interminables, où vous donnez un tas de détails qui certes intéressent vos amies, mais aucunement votre homme. Votre homme ne veut pas connaître tous les dessous de l'affaire, il cherche seulement à savoir ce que vous voulez.

Si vous voulez qu'il vous raconte sa journée au bureau, posez-lui des questions courtes mais précises, comme : « Le projet X est-il terminé ? » ou « Avez-vous trouvé quelqu'un pour combler le poste ? », etc. Ne lui demandez pas comment s'est passée sa journée, car il vous répondra que ça a été une bonne ou une mauvaise journée, point. Veillez aussi à préciser pourquoi vous voulez le savoir : par exemple, parce que vous vous intéressez à ce qu'il fait ou parce que vous l'aimez. Quelle que soit votre intention, c'est ce qui donne le prétexte qu'il faut à votre homme pour parler.

Mais attention, *tous* les hommes trouvent les femmes compliquées, et chaque fois qu'une femme pose une question à son homme, il se sent immédiatement pris au piège. Il est sur la défensive et cherche désespérément à savoir quelle est l'intention derrière la question et se creuse la tête pour trouver la bonne réponse : celle que la femme veut entendre. Si vous ne voulez pas que votre homme se sente pris au piège chaque fois que vous lui posez une question, manifestez-lui votre intention dès le départ.

Donc, lorsque vous demandez quelque chose à votre homme, indiquez-lui dès le départ le *but de votre question*, *l'utilité de votre question* ainsi que *votre intention*.

Soyez claire et précise, ne vous perdez pas dans un flot de mots et n'abordez qu'un seul sujet à la fois. L'homme aime bien vider une question avant de passer à une autre. Souvenez-vous-en.

Si vous êtes trop vague dans votre façon de poser la question, vous ne réussirez pas à attirer son attention. Il n'aura pas envie de vous écouter ni de vous parler et se mettra sur la défensive, car il ne comprendra pas *pourquoi* vous lui demandez cela.

Bref, ne lui parlez pas de façon qu'il doive lire entre les lignes pour vous comprendre. L'homme n'a pas appris à lire de cette façon, et comme l'intuition n'est pas son fort, vous risquez de ne jamais être comprise si vous ne lui parlez pas clairement. Qui a dit que ce sont les femmes qui étaient compliquées?

Lorsque vous posez une question à votre homme, êtes-vous satisfaite de sa réponse?

«*Si je lui demande l'heure, en général, oui. Pour le reste, on peut repasser. Il faut vraiment que ça soit simple et qu'il n'ait pas à trop développer sa réponse pour que ça sonne "correct".*»

Anabelle, 26 ans

«*Oui, si ma question est très claire. Sinon, je la reformule autrement, je me mets à son "niveau". Ça dépend vraiment des hommes, ils ne sont pas tous pareils. Les gais comprennent plus vite, en général.*»

Fanny, 32 ans

«Non, parce que la plupart du temps, il ne me répond pas. Alors, je m'arrange toute seule. Parfois, je me dis que je serais peut-être mieux si je vivais seule. Cela me ferait un enfant de moins... »

Christiane, 29 ans

—————<◦>—————

«Non. Il faut toujours lui répéter la question une fois ou deux pour avoir une réponse «valable». C'est pas toujours vite, ces petites bêtes-là ! »

Solange, 37 ans

—————<◦>—————

« Quand la question est simple, oui. Si la question est complexe, je la divise en petites sous-questions, pour lui donner une chance. »

Mariska, 41 ans

—————<◦>—————

« Oui, parce que je pose les questions directement, sans détour. Autrement, il ne comprend pas. »

Angela, 24 ans

—————<◦>—————

Règle n° 3

L'homme parle si c'est utile

Pour parler, l'homme a besoin d'un pré-texte, la femme n'a besoin que d'une occasion.

Pour faire parler son homme, la femme doit prendre l'initiative de la conversation, en ayant à l'esprit que l'homme n'aime pas parler juste pour le plaisir. S'il y a un but à la conversation, votre homme sera heureux d'échanger avec vous. Si vous le forcez à parler sans raison valable à ses yeux, ses idées se mêleront dans sa tête, il se sentira menacé et attaqué, et il ne dira rien car il aura besoin de réfléchir.

Attaquer son homme de front pour le faire parler aura pour résultat qu'il ira se réfugier dans ses quartiers, dans son silence. Plus vous lui forcerez la main, plus il évitera tout échange avec vous.

L'homme s'exprimera de lui-même pour deux raisons : soit pour faire des reproches, soit pour demander de l'information. Donc, quand la femme déballe ses ennuis, l'homme y verra des reproches, une demande d'information ou une solution. Il croira cela parce qu'il est comme cela.

Plus l'homme assaille sa femme d'informations et de solutions, plus elle les écarte en continuant son bla-bla, plus l'homme cherche à se retirer de la conversation car il se sent inutile ; il ne voit pas pourquoi elle lui dit tout cela si elle ne veut pas de son aide. Dites-lui dès le départ que vous voulez seulement être écoutée et que vous ne lui faites pas de reproches, vous éviterez ainsi bien des malentendus et personne ne se sentira incompris ou rejeté.

Deux femmes peuvent parler de tout et de rien pendant des heures. Elles n'ont besoin que d'un « comment ça va ? » pour amorcer une longue conversation sur tout ce qui leur passe par la tête.

Les hommes sont différents. Lorsque l'homme parle, il doit savoir où la conversation va le mener ; pourquoi et de quoi il va parler, si c'est utile et de combien de temps il dispose pour le faire. Si vous voulez que votre homme vous parle, posez-lui une question précise, sur un seul sujet à la fois, et informez-le du temps dont vous disposez pour cette conversation. Et, surtout, exprimez-lui clairement que vous avez besoin de sa réponse.

Pour l'homme, il est facile de séparer tous les aspects de sa vie, tandis que pour la femme les aspects de la vie forment un tout et sont indissociables. Pour l'homme, le travail n'a rien à voir avec la vie de couple, la vie de couple n'a rien à voir avec les amis, les amis n'ont rien à voir avec la vie de famille, etc. Il juge donc inutile de parler de son travail à sa compagne quand il rentre à la maison, puisque pour lui cela ne la concerne pas.

L'homme n'a pas besoin de raconter sa journée pour vivre un moment d'intimité avec sa compagne. Sa simple présence lui permet ce moment d'intimité.

L'homme a besoin d'une raison pour s'exprimer. Il pense en fonction des solutions et ne voit pas du tout l'intérêt de partager le processus de pensée qui l'a mené à cette solution.

Si vous voulez faire parler votre homme, donnez-lui une bonne raison de le faire. Si vous voulez seulement être écoutée, dites-le-lui. Si vous voulez qu'il vous aide à trouver une solution à un problème, dites-le-lui. Ne l'assommez pas avec tous vos ennuis, allez-y avec une seule chose à la fois et donnez-lui le temps d'y penser. Plus vous insisterez pour le faire parler, moins il parlera car il croira que vous cherchez à le manipuler et se sentira pris au piège.

S'il sent qu'il peut être utile, non seulement il vous écoutera, mais il vous parlera aussi. Manifestez votre intention dès le départ et vous éviterez des frustrations et des disputes inutiles. N'oubliez pas de le remercier lorsqu'il vous écoute et lorsqu'il vous parle. Cela peut sembler exagéré, mais en le remerciant, vous le rassurez dans son rôle de héros et de bon compagnon dont vous ne pouvez pas vous passer. Et pour lui, c'est là une excellente raison de vous écouter et de vous parler. Si une femme fait sentir à son homme qu'il est utile, il fera tout pour montrer à sa compagne qu'elle a raison de le voir ainsi.

Votre homme doit absolument sentir qu'il est indispensable à vos yeux pour répondre à vos besoins. Si vous ne lui dites pas que vous l'aimez tel qu'il est, qu'il vous satisfait, qu'il est un bon compagnon, votre homme se sentira vite inutile et ne fera rien pour vous satisfaire, parce qu'il croit que vous n'avez pas besoin de lui, que vous ne le jugez pas assez bon. Si votre homme ne sent pas que vous lui faites confiance, s'il sent que vous le croyez incapable, il ne fera plus rien pour ne pas vous décevoir encore plus. Qui a dit que les hommes étaient sûrs d'eux ?

Au quotidien, qu'est-ce que votre homme vous demande ? De quoi vous parle-t-il sans que vous ayez demandé quoi que ce soit ?

« Il me demande toujours où j'ai mis ses affaires. Il aime aussi beaucoup me parler de ses performances sportives. Je trouve ça plate à mort, mais ça lui fait tellement plaisir de croire que ça m'impressionne ! »

Anabelle, 26 ans

« En général, il ne me demande pas grand-chose. Il est plutôt autonome et déteste que je me mêle de ses affaires d'homme, comme si j'étais incompétente dans tout ce qui le concerne... »

Fanny, 32 ans

« Il me demande des trucs banals, mais il ne me pose jamais de questions profondes ou intimes. Je pense que ça ne l'intéresse tout simplement pas. »

Christiane, 29 ans

———◦———

« Pour tout ce qui concerne la maison, j'ai vraiment l'impression qu'il ne sait rien. Il me demande souvent où se trouvent les enfants, la télécommande, le beurre, ses bas, etc. J'ai vraiment l'impression, parfois, qu'il est un peu "épais". Il ne se rappelle jamais ce que je lui ai dit. J'ai même l'impression parfois qu'il est pire qu'un enfant. En tout cas, il me demande autant d'attention que nos enfants. »

Solange, 37 ans

———◦———

« Il ne me demande jamais rien d'important. Ça porte toujours sur des détails insignifiants. Ah ! mais la fois où j'ai égratigné la voiture, j'ai eu droit à tout un interrogatoire ! »

Mariska, 41 ans

———◦———

« Il me demande souvent si je suis contente d'être avec lui. J'essaie de le rassurer, mais j'ai l'impression que c'est toujours à recommencer. »

Angela, 24 ans

———◦———

Règle nº 4

Un problème
= une solution

Pour l'homme, l'émotion exprime un problème ou un conflit. Lorsque sa partenaire est émotive, il voit donc là un problème ou un conflit. Sachez que l'homme n'exprime pas ses émotions comme une femme. S'il a un problème, il va s'arranger pour le régler tout seul. Il n'a pas besoin d'aide, et s'il en a besoin il vous le dira. Mais il tentera d'abord de régler ses problèmes tout seul, pour vous prouver et se prouver à lui-même qu'il est capable de le faire. Vous demander de l'aide pour des choses importantes sera vraiment son dernier recours. Pour l'homme, demander de l'aide, c'est avouer sa vulnérabilité et son incapacité, et il craindra que vous n'ayez plus confiance en lui s'il n'est pas capable de se débrouiller tout seul. Pire encore, si vous insistez pour l'aider, il croira immédiatement que vous le jugez incapable, incompétent, et conclura que vous n'avez pas besoin de lui.

Cependant, votre homme n'aura pas du tout cette attitude en ce qui concerne les petites choses du quotidien. Par exemple, il pourra vous demander vingt fois par jour où vous avez mis telle ou telle chose. Il ne craindra pas d'avoir l'air incompétent pour ces petits détails qu'il juge banals. Mais pour ce qui a trait aux choses importantes, il voudra absolument se débrouiller tout seul.

L'homme peut demander de l'aide pour de petites choses, mais pour les autres il aime se débrouiller seul pour vous prouver que vous pouvez compter sur lui, qu'il est compétent, bref, qu'il est votre héros! L'homme ne comprend pas que s'il parle de ses problèmes à sa partenaire, elle ne le jugera pas incompétent. Il veut trouver une solution, l'appliquer et, ensuite, il vous en parlera peut-être. Parce qu'il croit avoir réponse à tous les problèmes, il ne vous demandera pas de l'aider. Régler les choses, réparer, arranger, cela fait partie de son travail de mâle, de bon compagnon, de héros. Vouloir prendre sa place en essayant de lui apporter une aide sans qu'il l'ait sollicitée, c'est lui signifier qu'il ne fait pas son travail correctement, qu'il est incompétent.

Vous ne pouvez pas aider votre homme s'il ne veut pas être aidé. Quand il vit quelque chose, il sait qu'il ressent des émotions mais il ne peut les identifier clairement. Il est donc très difficile pour lui de les exprimer. Il préfère garder pour lui ce qu'il ressent et tenter de régler ses problèmes sans étaler ses états d'âme à qui que ce soit. Il ne veut pas identifier ses émotions, et encore moins les exprimer; il veut seulement régler le problème.

Les hommes sont aussi sensibles que les femmes, sauf qu'ils ne savent pas comment exprimer leur sensibilité. Si la femme sait souvent ce que ressent son homme sans qu'il ait prononcé un mot, l'inverse est tout à fait inconcevable.

La femme, lorsqu'elle communique avec l'homme, lui parle comme s'il était sa meilleure amie et elle s'attend donc à ce qu'il réagisse comme le ferait sa meilleure amie. Mais l'homme n'est pas sa meilleure amie, et il ne se confie même pas à ses meilleurs amis à lui, pas plus qu'il ne reçoit de confidences de leur part. Pourquoi donc ferait-il avec sa conjointe ce qu'il ne fait avec personne d'autre ?

Les amitiés féminines et les amitiés masculines sont très différentes. Lorsqu'ils se rencontrent, les hommes agissent. Les femmes, elles, parlent. L'homme est intime avec quelqu'un par le simple fait qu'il est présent. De son côté, la femme se sent intime avec quelqu'un lorsqu'il y a échange verbal. L'homme n'a pas besoin de parler pour se sentir intime avec quelqu'un, contrairement à la femme, pour qui c'est essentiel. C'est pourquoi les hommes vont jouer au golf ensemble tandis que les femmes vont au restaurant.

Pour être intime avec une femme, l'homme ne sent aucunement le besoin de parler de sa vie en détail, de ses problèmes, de ses joies ou de ce qu'il fait de ses journées. Il n'est donc pas étonnant que lorsqu'une femme se confie à son homme, elle se sent incomprise car il ne lui rend pas la pareille.

Si vous voulez que votre homme vous confie ses problèmes, faites-lui sentir qu'il est merveilleux, indispensable, compétent, et que peu importe ce qui lui arrive vous aurez toujours confiance en lui. Autant qu'une femme, sinon plus, l'homme a besoin d'être rassuré pour donner le meilleur de lui-même et pour en arriver quelquefois à se confier, voire à se faire aider.

Du point de vue de l'homme, la femme qui lui confie un problème lui donne par le fait même le mandat de trouver une solution. Il ne vous écoutera pas comme le ferait une copine, car il croit que vous lui demandez de l'aide ou que vous le tenez responsable du problème. Il s'affairera donc à trouver une solution au lieu de se contenter de vous écouter.

Lorsque la femme fait des confidences à son conjoint, il se sent immédiatement concerné directement, voire responsable. Il ne réagira pas comme la femme le souhaite, il sera plutôt sur la défensive et tentera de s'en sortir par tous les moyens possibles, cherchant rapidement la solution parfaite.

Lorsque la femme exprime ses problèmes à son conjoint, elle lui lance un message d'amour et de confiance, mais l'homme ne le reçoit pas du tout de cette façon. Il croit qu'il est responsable du problème puisque sa femme lui en parle. Il est donc tout de suite sur ses gardes et la bombarde de solutions. Or, la femme ne veut pas de solution, elle veut seulement être écoutée. Mais l'homme est convaincu qu'il fait partie du problème et qu'il doit trouver une solution ; sans cela, pourquoi lui en parlerait-elle ?

Si vous sentez que votre homme est réticent à vous écouter, c'est sûrement parce que vous ne vous y êtes pas prise correctement. Si vous faites sentir à votre homme qu'il fait partie de la solution et non du problème, il vous apportera toute son aide et tout son appui.

La femme ferait mieux de garder ses confidences pour son prochain « souper de filles » (ou pour son ami gai, si elle tient absolument à en parler avec un homme) si elle veut qu'on l'écoute et qu'on lui apporte la réponse immédiate qu'elle attend lorsqu'elle s'exprime.

Si vous voulez lui raconter vos ennuis ou votre journée, dites-lui dès le départ que vous voulez seulement qu'il vous écoute, que cela vous fait du bien et que vous savez qu'il peut le faire. Il y a fort à parier qu'il vous écoutera sans chercher des solutions pour vous et sera attentif à vos propos. Vous pouvez aussi lui préciser qu'il n'est pas responsable de vos ennuis. Cela le soulagera et le mettra dans d'excellentes dispositions pour vous écouter et peut-être même pour vous parler à son tour.

Votre homme vous parle-t-il de ses problèmes ?
Vous demande-t-il de l'aider ?

« *Jamais. Il est beaucoup trop orgueilleux pour cela.* »

Anabelle, 26 ans

«*En général, non. Je crois qu'il ne me trouve pas assez compétente pour l'aider, pour les choses importantes du moins. Pour les petites choses du quotidien, je suis indispensable.*»

Fanny, 32 ans

———◦———

«*Rarement. Je crois qu'il préfère s'organiser tout seul. Et en ne me parlant pas, il évite de répondre à mes questions ou d'avoir à me rendre des comptes.*»

Christiane, 29 ans

———◦———

«*Jamais. Il m'en parle seulement une fois qu'il a tout réglé. Ça m'énerve, car j'ai l'impression qu'il m'exclut, qu'il vit à deux endroits.*»

Solange, 37 ans

———◦———

«*Il ne me demande jamais rien d'important, c'est toujours des niaiseries du genre "combien on met de savon dans le lave-vaisselle ?". Mais quand il s'agit de trouver des solutions à mes problèmes, il a toujours quelque chose à dire.*»

Mariska, 41 ans

———◦———

«*Oui, mais c'est rare. Quand il me demande de l'aide, c'est qu'il est vraiment à court de solutions. Souvent, il préfère courir à l'échec... Ah! l'orgueil du mâle!*»

Angela, 24 ans

———◦———

46

Règle n° 5

Acceptez ses réponses

Quand vous posez une question à votre homme, vous voulez entendre sa réponse. Ne soyez pas offusquée s'il ne répond pas ce que vous vouliez entendre. Vous avez posé la question, vous devez être prête à assumer toutes les réponses, même celles qui vous déplaisent. Rappelez-vous, l'homme n'est pas comme vous, il ne voit pas que vous cherchez une approbation, du réconfort, si vous ne lui avez pas dit au départ. Il vous répond donc comme seul un homme peut le faire, sans passer par quatre chemins, avec une solution toute prête qui devrait, en principe, vous suffire car il a réglé votre problème. Il ne voit pas les consé-quences de sa réponse. Selon lui, il a fait son travail, il a exprimé la réponse qu'il jugeait la plus adéquate. Votre homme ne répond pas à vos questions pour vous faire de la peine ou pour avoir le dessus sur vous, il le fait parce que vous lui avez posé une question. Contrairement aux femmes, les hommes ne font pas de sous-entendus, ils ne passent pas de messages à décoder entre les lignes. Ils disent ce qu'ils ont à dire, un point, c'est tout.

Votre homme ne pense pas qu'il pourrait répondre en fonction de ce que vous ressentez et de ce que vous pensez, il cherche seulement à vous donner la réponse la plus correcte et la plus honnête possible compte tenu des informations dont il dispose. Encore une fois, si vous ne lui dites pas ce que vous attendez de lui, ne comptez pas sur lui pour le deviner.

Ce que l'homme craint le plus chez une femme, c'est sa capacité incroyable de se souvenir de tout ce qu'il lui a confié dans le passé. Mais attention, si vous vous servez des confidences qu'il vous a faites pour chercher à avoir raison, soyez sûre que votre homme ne se confiera plus jamais à vous. Si vous cherchez à utiliser ses confidences contre lui, chaque fois que vous lui demanderez quelque chose, il y verra un piège et ne se commettra pas.

Le simple fait de lui remettre sous le nez des choses qu'il vous a dites au cours de disputes ou des confidences qu'il vous a faites, et ce, pour faire valoir votre point de vue ou pour lui prouver que vous avez raison, amènera votre homme à fuir toute discussion avec vous.

Lui reprocher ses réponses et remettre en question ses confidences, c'est comme lui reprocher de ne pas être à la hauteur, de ne pas vous satisfaire.

Si vous n'apprenez pas à voir ses réponses pour ce qu'elles sont, et non pour des attaques personnelles visant à vous blesser, votre homme commencera à vous répondre de façon évasive ou même à vous mentir pour ne pas vous offusquer et vous donner d'autres armes pour l'attaquer. Se servir des réponses et des confidences de votre homme pour chercher à avoir le dessus sur lui, c'est le meilleur moyen de le faire taire à jamais.

Par exemple, si vous lui demandez s'il trouve que vous avez engraissé et qu'il vous répond que oui, ne vous en prenez pas à lui. Ce n'est certes pas délicat de sa part, mais il a au moins le mérite d'être honnête. Et s'il ne vous a jamais parlé du fait que vous ayez engraissé, c'est sans doute qu'il s'en fiche. Il l'a remarqué, et après? Il vous en a parlé uniquement parce que vous lui avez posé la question. Il vous aime toujours, il vous désire tout autant. Ce n'est pas lui que ça dérange, c'est vous.

Si sa réponse vous fait de la peine, exprimez-lui votre peine, votre crainte qu'il ne vous trouve plus aussi belle, mais dites-lui surtout quelle importance cela a pour vous. Votre homme sera plus enclin à vous rassurer s'il sait que c'est important pour vous,.

Toute question sur votre apparence physique devrait être exprimée seulement si vous remarquez un changement d'attitude du côté de votre conjoint. S'il agit comme il agissait quand vous pesiez quelques kilos de moins, c'est qu'il vous aime et vous désire tout autant, et se fiche complètement de votre prise de poids. Il est même fort probable qu'il ne l'ait pas remarqué...

S'il rigole de vos ennuis, rigolez avec lui. Il ne le fait pas parce qu'il vous trouve ridicule, mais simplement pour vous aider à dédramatiser la situation. Si pour vous le sujet est trop sérieux pour en rire, dites-lui gentiment que cela vous tient à cœur et que si ce n'est pas le bon moment pour en parler, vous pouvez remettre cette conversation à un moment plus opportun.

L'homme est plus physique et plus intellectuel que la femme, qui, pour sa part, est plus émotive et plus spirituelle que lui. C'est pourquoi l'homme cherche à vous raisonner lorsque vous exprimez vos émotions, et il le fait uniquement pour mieux comprendre ce que vous vivez. La femme peut donc avoir l'impression que son homme ne comprend pas ce qu'elle lui dit et qu'il cherche à avoir raison à tout prix. Or, votre homme ne cherche pas à avoir le dernier mot, il veut seulement vous aider et, surtout, vous prouver qu'il est compétent et qu'il peut vous sauver. Ce n'est pas sa faute : il veut bien faire, et fait ce qu'il sait faire de mieux, c'est-à-dire vous donner des solutions toute faites. Dans sa tête, le problème est réglé dès qu'il a trouvé un moyen de le régler, et il ne comprend pas pourquoi vous continuez d'en parler. Il vous a donné une solution, après tout.

Soyez compréhensive et essayez de lui parler à son «niveau». Autrement dit, soyez un peu plus cérébrale. Cela ne veut pas dire éliminer toute émotion de votre propos, mais seulement y intégrer un peu plus de raison, si l'on peut dire.

Pendant que la femme exprime des émotions, l'homme recueille des informations de façon à lui apporter une solution. Soyez consciente de ce processus mental typiquement mâle et expliquez-lui (clairement et de façon concise) que vous avez besoin d'exprimer quelque chose, sans toujours vouloir l'expliquer. Et que s'il ne voit pas où vous voulez en venir, il peut simplement se taire et vous écouter en vous apportant du réconfort; cela vous suffira. S'il sait cela, votre homme sera tout ouïe et s'efforcera de vous parler pour vous faire du bien et non pour vous dire comment régler vos problèmes.

Une fois cela compris par les deux partenaires, la communication devient beaucoup plus simple, agréable et constructive pour le couple. Accepter les différences qui existent entre l'homme et la femme, c'est le premier pas pour mieux se comprendre.

Vous arrive-t-il d'être déçue des réponses ou des commentaires de votre homme?

«*Presque toujours. J'ai l'impression qu'il ne comprend pas ce que j'attends de lui.*»

Anabelle, 26 ans

«*En général, non. Je prends ce qu'il me dit pour ce que c'est et je finis toujours par en faire à ma tête, sans tenir trop compte de ce qu'il pense.*»

Fanny, 32 ans

———————◄○►———————

« *Toujours. J'ai l'impression qu'il croit que je suis incapable de régler les problèmes toute seule. Pourtant, s'il savait tout ce que je fais dans une journée, il épargnerait sa salive.* »

Christiane, 29 ans

———————◄○►———————

« *Presque toujours. Si j'ai besoin d'une information, c'est magique, il peut me parler pendant des heures. Mais quand il s'agit seulement de me soutenir (avec les enfants surtout), c'est une autre histoire. Parfois, je me dis que ça ne ferait pas une grande différence si j'étais seule.* »

Solange, 37 ans

———————◄○►———————

« *Souvent, il ne comprend pas ce que j'attends de lui. Ses réponses sont tellement vagues que j'aurais pu obtenir les mêmes d'un étranger. Je pense qu'il a peur de me montrer qu'il n'est pas parfait. Comme si je ne le savais pas !* »

Mariska, 41 ans

———————◄○►———————

« *Oui. Il ne répond jamais vraiment à mes questions. Il essaie de me dire quoi faire au lieu d'essayer de comprendre comment je me sens.* »

Angela, 24 ans

———————◄○►———————

Règle n° 6

Laissez-le parler sans l'accuser de le faire!

Souvent, la femme reproche à son homme de ne pas s'exprimer mais, quand il le fait, elle lui reproche de trop parler et de vouloir avoir le dernier mot. Pourtant, tout ce qu'il tente de faire, c'est ce qu'elle veut qu'il fasse: s'exprimer! Lorsque l'homme se confie à la femme, celle-ci a tendance à l'interrompre parce qu'il ne lui dit pas ce qu'elle voudrait entendre. Mais interrompre son homme, c'est le meilleur moyen de le faire taire.

L'homme ne peut faire deux choses en même temps; il ne peut donc exprimer ses émotions tout en tenant compte des vôtres. Lorsque vous réagissez à chaque phrase ou à chaque intonation pendant que votre homme vous parle, vous prenez vraiment le risque de l'agacer. Il est déjà difficile pour lui de s'exprimer, car il a besoin de toute sa concentration. L'interrompre, c'est risquer de le mêler, et que fait l'homme quand il est mêlé? Il se réfugie dans le silence.

Pour une fois qu'il vous parle, donnez-vous la peine de l'écouter sans rien dire. Si vous l'interrompez, vous ajouterez des éléments nouveaux à la discussion et il croira que vous cherchez à le coincer et à le faire passer pour un incapable ou un incompétent.

Contrairement à la femme, l'homme aborde un sujet à la fois et vide complètement la question. Si vous l'interrompez, il croira que ce qu'il dit n'est pas correct, qu'il n'a pas la bonne réponse, qu'il a tort. Il montera donc le ton pour faire valoir son point de vue et la discussion risquera de tourner en dispute. Pire, il pourrait vous donner raison pour mettre fin à la discussion.

Pour la femme qui discute avec son homme, il est plus difficile d'écouter que de parler. Si le sujet n'intéresse pas la femme, elle ne sera pas portée à écouter. Pourtant, dans le couple, une bonne écoute est à la source d'une bonne communication. Et si vous arrivez à bien écouter votre homme, il s'efforcera de vous rendre la pareille.

Évitez de réagir à un mot, à un geste ou à une intonation quand votre homme vous parle. Laissez-le plutôt dire tout ce qu'il a à dire, jusqu'au bout, sans l'interrompre. Lorsqu'il aura terminé, demandez-lui s'il a fini et, avant de lui répondre, résumez ce qu'il vient de vous dire et demandez-lui si vous avez bien compris.

Évitez de l'accuser de tous les maux parce qu'il n'a pas répondu «correctement» à votre question. Au lieu de lui dire qu'il n'a rien compris ou qu'il ne vous a pas écoutée, précisez-lui ce que vous voulez réellement savoir en lui posant une autre question ou en lui demandant d'ajouter des détails ou de préciser sa pensée.

Quand votre homme vous parle, ce n'est pas le moment de l'interrompre et encore moins de l'accuser de s'exprimer comme il le fait. Cela lui demande déjà beaucoup d'effort, car il se sent vulnérable. Si en plus sa compagne le désapprouve, il pourrait se montrer très agacé et se mettre en colère. Ou alors, vous donner raison et se taire. Et c'est bien connu, si chaque fois que votre homme vous parle vous l'accusez de tous les torts et lui reprochez ses réponses, il ne vous parlera plus de peur de vous décevoir à nouveau. L'homme est sensible, et il est facile de le mettre à terre quand il est vulnérable, c'est-à-dire quand il vous parle, quand il se confie.

Écoutez donc votre homme jusqu'au bout. Même si ce qu'il vous dit n'a aucun rapport avec ce que vous lui avez demandé ou si c'est si ennuyant qu'un insomniaque tomberait endormi, il s'exprime ! Écoutez-le sans lui souffler les réponses ; c'est lui qui doit parler et non vous à travers lui. Une fois qu'il a terminé et que vous avez confirmé que c'est bien le cas, vérifiez si vous avez bien compris son propos au lieu de risquer de l'interpréter de travers. Vous éviterez ainsi de créer un froid et d'entamer une dispute inutile. Dans l'art de la parole, les hommes ne sont pas aussi doués que les femmes. Ils ont encore bien des choses à apprendre.

Quand votre homme vous parle, montrez-lui que vous êtes intéressée par ses propos, par exemple en hochant la tête, en le touchant ou en faisant « hum, hum », « ah oui ! », etc. L'idée ici n'est pas de lui dire que vous êtes d'accord avec tout ce qu'il vous dit, mais que vous l'écoutez attentivement et que vous tentez de comprendre ce qu'il vous dit. Vous l'encouragerez ainsi à parler et il s'en souviendra à l'avenir.

Mettre en pratique cette règle n'est pas toujours facile, avouons-le, mais elle peut faire des miracles pour ce qui est d'encourager votre homme à vous parler. À la longue, il pourrait même vous confier ses plus grands secrets, car il sait que vous l'écoutez sincèrement, que vous lui faites confiance et que vous appréciez qu'il vous parle.

Comment réagissez-vous lorsque votre homme se confie à vous ? Quels sont vos gestes ? Que dites-vous ?

« Je l'écoute le plus possible, mais je ne comprends pas toujours où il veut en venir. »

Anabelle, 26 ans

« J'essaie de lui montrer que je suis intéressée par ce qu'il me dit, mais j'ai tendance à l'interrompre parce que je ne vois pas toujours le but de ses explications. »

Fanny, 32 ans

« Je l'écoute la plupart du temps, mais j'ai souvent l'impression qu'il est en train de se justifier et alors j'essaie de trouver pourquoi il le fait. Il me parle souvent comme s'il avait quelque chose à me cacher. »

Christiane, 29 ans

———<o>———

« Je lui coupe la parole ! Sinon, ça n'a pas de fin ! Et il n'y a jamais moyen de discuter avec lui, il veut toujours avoir raison ! »

Solange, 37 ans

———<o>———

« Je fais semblant de l'écouter la plupart du temps, surtout si ça n'a pas trop d'importance. Il croit que je l'écoute attentivement parce que je le laisse finir sans rien dire. Il ne sait pas que j'ai parfois la tête ailleurs. »

Mariska, 41 ans

———<o>———

« Je l'écoute en essayant de me mettre à sa place et j'essaie de ne pas trop critiquer ce qu'il me dit, mais parfois, je n'ai pas le choix parce qu'il est vraiment trop con. »

Angela, 24 ans

———<o>———

Règle n° 7

Ne répondez pas à sa place

Répondre à la place de son homme, c'est jouer le rôle de la mère avec lui. Dès que vous répondez à la place de votre homme, vous lui dites qu'il est incompétent et que ça ne sert à rien qu'il vous parle puisque vous ne le considérez pas capable de le faire. Il reçoit comme message que vous ne le sentez pas apte à répondre correctement et il s'abstiendra dès lors de le faire. Pour être efficace et actif dans votre vie de couple, votre homme a besoin de sentir que vous l'admirez. Si vous le faites sentir incompétent en répondant à sa place, il croira que vous ne l'admirez plus et qu'il n'est pas à la hauteur. Votre homme veut être votre héros, il veut sentir que vous avez besoin de lui. Répondre à sa place lui envoie le message contraire. Votre homme a besoin de sentir que vous l'approuvez, que vous lui faites confiance, que vous tenez à lui. Il est très important pour l'homme de sentir que sa compagne lui fait confiance, et ne pas répondre à sa place, c'est lui dire qu'il a de la valeur, que vous le trouvez intelligent, intéressant, et que vous savez qu'il peut se débrouiller tout seul.

Écoutez-le comme vous aimeriez qu'il vous écoute, c'est-à-dire en le laissant parler. Même si sa réponse ne vous plaît pas, abstenez-vous de le reprendre. Il répond au meilleur de sa conscience, et cette réponse vient de lui. Rejeter sa réponse en lui en imposant une autre, c'est le rejeter, lui.

S'il ne sait pas quoi répondre quand une tierce personne lui pose une question et qu'il veut que vous l'aidiez, il vous fera signe, et alors, mais seulement alors, vous pourrez répondre à sa place. Prenez soin, si vous le faites, d'utiliser le «je», en disant par exemple: «Je crois que mon conjoint apprécierait que vous veniez à ce rendez-vous, c'est bien cela, chéri?» C'est le moment d'utiliser votre sixième sens pour répondre ce qu'il aurait lui-même répondu. En lui demandant, après cela, si c'est bien cela qu'il aurait dit, vous lui ouvrez la voie pour qu'il puisse s'exprimer comme le grand garçon autonome qu'il est et poursuivre la conversation sans votre aide. Vous lui montrez que vous l'aidez mais que vous le laissez diriger l'aide que vous lui apportez. Il vous sera alors très reconnaissant de ne pas prendre toute la place et, de ce fait, de ne pas remettre en question ses capacités et ses compétences.

Et si sa réponse tarde à venir, n'avancez pas de réponse pour lui à moins qu'il ne vous ait clairement fait signe de le faire. Vous ne savez pas ce qui se passe dans sa tête, tout comme vous ne pouvez savoir ce qui se passe dans la tête de quiconque. Vous ne pouvez pas prédire ce qu'il va répondre, puisque vous ne le savez pas. Et si vous le savez, eh bien, laissez-le lui-même vous confirmer que vous aviez raison, sans lui dire toutefois que vous le saviez, car cela lui ferait le même effet que si vous aviez répondu à sa place.

L'homme est délicat, et il faut savoir le ménager. Il ne l'admettra jamais, certes, mais maintenant que vous le savez, vous avez une carte de plus dans votre jeu. Cependant, ne lui dites jamais cela, vous perdriez tout votre pouvoir.

Vous arrive-t-il de répondre à la place de votre conjoint ? Dans quelles circonstances ? Pourquoi le faites-vous ?

« Ça m'arrive souvent, parce qu'il n'est pas toujours vite, vite... »

Anabelle, 26 ans

« Parfois, oui, quand je sens qu'il ne sait pas quoi dire parce qu'il ne comprend pas ce qu'on attend de lui. »

Fanny, 32 ans

« *Oui, souvent, quand je sais qu'il ne sait pas quoi dire ou qu'il va dire une connerie. Je préfère répondre à sa place. C'est souvent moins embarrassant.* »

Solange, 37 ans

─────◄○►─────

« *Oui, quand je le laisse faire, il se perd dans une explication interminable qui ennuie tout le monde. Quand je réponds pour lui, je ne lui rends peut-être pas service, mais je rends service aux autres.* »

Christiane, 29 ans

─────◄○►─────

« *Oui, quand je sens qu'il est mal pris. Mais la plupart du temps, je le laisse se démerder tout seul, même s'il se met un pied dans la bouche une fois sur deux. C'est son problème, pas le mien.* »

Mariska, 41 ans

─────◄○►─────

« *Souvent, si je le laisse parler, je sais qu'il va dire des conneries. Je le laisse répondre tout seul quand ce n'est pas important, mais pour les choses "officielles", je préfère parler à sa place. Ça nous évite de perdre du temps et de l'énergie à tenter de faire comprendre ce qu'il veut réellement dire.* »

Angela, 24 ans

─────◄○►─────

Règle n° 8

Passez du vouloir au pouvoir

> *« Le moindre soupçon d'exigence dans le ton de votre voix sera interprété pour l'homme comme un reproche à son endroit. Et puisqu'il semble que ses efforts ne vous suffisent pas, il les réduira jusqu'à ce que vous lui paraissiez apprécier à sa juste valeur tout ce qu'il a déjà fait pour vous. »*

John Gray

L'homme ressent le besoin profond d'être accepté et admiré par sa partenaire. En exigeant des choses de lui au lieu de les lui demander, vous lui dites que vous le jugez incompétent, qu'il n'en fait pas assez et qu'il « est » le problème. Chaque exigence de votre part sera perçue par votre homme comme une critique. Si vous désirez qu'il prenne soin de vous et fasse des choses pour vous, il doit sentir que vous l'admirez et que vous avez confiance en lui, et ce, inconditionnellement.

Si vous demandez à votre homme s'il *voudrait* vous rendre service et qu'il vous répond non, vous le prenez de façon personnelle parce qu'il vous a dit qu'il ne *voulait* pas vous aider. Si, en revanche, vous lui demandez s'il *pourrait* vous rendre service et qu'il vous répond non, cela n'aura pas du tout le même impact sur vous. En effet, qu'il ne *puisse* et qu'il ne *veuille* pas sont des choses bien différentes.

Quand vous demandez à votre homme s'il *peut* vous aider, vous rendre service, vous faites appel à ses capacités et à ses compétences. Il ne se sentira donc pas obligé de le faire, mais il le fera, la plupart du temps, car il a le choix et qu'il sait que cela va vous aider. Qu'il *puisse* vous rendre service lui donne le sentiment profond d'être utile et d'être un bon compagnon pour vous. Il se sent indispensable. Enfin, vous le prenez pour le héros qu'il est !

Lorsque vous voulez lui parler d'un problème que vous avez, exprimez-le-lui en une courte phrase et dites-lui que vous aimeriez savoir ce qu'il ferait à votre place. Il vous demandera alors plus d'informations afin de trouver la meilleure solution pour vous, et vous aurez avec lui une vraie conversation.

Si vous faites appel à ses compétences, à son savoir, il verra tout de suite où vous voulez en venir et n'hésitera pas à s'exprimer abondamment sur le sujet car il connaîtra le but de cette conversation. Elle ne sera pas inutile et il y accordera donc de l'énergie et du temps.

Pour arriver à donner le meilleur de soi-même, la femme a besoin de se sentir aimée, et l'homme, lui, doit sentir qu'on a besoin de lui. Si l'homme ne se sent plus essentiel ou indispensable aux yeux de sa compagne, il deviendra vite distant, froid, voire indifférent. Lorsque l'homme se sent inutile aux yeux de celle qu'il aime, il agit de sorte qu'elle se sentira de moins en moins aimée, même si ce n'est pas du tout le cas.

Si le pauvre homme sent que vous ne l'admirez plus, que vous ne le voyez plus comme un héros, il s'éloignera de vous pour ne pas vous décevoir encore plus.

Pour obtenir ce que vous voulez de votre homme, demandez-lui s'il *peut* vous donner ce qu'il vous donne déjà. En le faisant, vous prendrez conscience de tout ce que votre homme fait pour vous et, doucement, vous pourrez ensuite y intégrer de nouvelles demandes.

Chaque fois que vous demandez quelque chose à votre homme, soyez prête à essuyer un refus et acceptez-le en lui répondant simplement «d'accord», sans insister. Puis, après avoir utilisé cette technique pendant quelque temps, ne dites plus rien lorsqu'il vous refuse quelque chose. Pas un mot, pas un grognement, pas un soupir: ne réagissez aucunement et poursuivez vos activités. Votre homme devrait alors se mettre à marmonner ou à grogner. Laissez-le faire sans mot dire et sans réagir. Il cherche un moyen de vous satisfaire et il y a fort à parier qu'il fera exactement ce que vous lui avez demandé. Pourquoi?

Parce que vous avez respecté son refus et n'y accordez aucune importance. Vous ne lui avez pas reproché son refus, pas plus que vous ne l'avez approuvé. En ne disant rien, vous avez laissé le problème entre ses mains, et comme il a naturellement tendance à trouver des solutions à tous les problèmes, il vous en donnera une. Bref, il fera ce que vous lui avez demandé. Tout ce que ces techniques demandent pour être efficaces, c'est un peu d'entraînement et de patience.

Si vous ne rejetez pas votre homme et si vous ne le punissez pas quand il vous refuse quelque chose, soyez sûre qu'il s'en souviendra la prochaine fois que vous lui demanderez son aide et qu'il sera très heureux de vous l'apporter. Et s'il ne *peut* pas faire quelque chose pour vous, ne tentez pas de lui prouver qu'il devrait le faire plus que vous; n'invoquez pas mille raisons lorsque vous lui demandez de vous rendre service. Soyez claire et concise, puis acceptez son refus le cas échéant.

Quand votre homme vous rend service, vous avez souvent l'impression qu'il vous fait une faveur, et vous n'avez pas tort. Mais pour votre homme, vous accorder une faveur, c'est vous prouver son amour, c'est vous dire à quel point il tient à vous.

Lorsque vous lui demandez quelque chose, soyez sûre qu'il ne verra pas là une preuve que vous n'en faites pas assez. Au contraire. Votre homme vous trouve si efficace et travaillante que, lorsque vous lui demandez un service, il est persuadé que vous avez vous-même donné beaucoup plus avant de lui demander quelque chose. Si c'est bien demandé, il sera heureux de faire sa part lui aussi.

Rappelez-vous, votre homme ne pense pas comme vous : il ne croit pas qu'il n'en fait jamais assez. Si vous ne lui demandez rien, il sera convaincu que tout est parfait et que ce qu'il fait pour vous vous satisfait au-delà de vos espérances. Dites-lui que vous avez besoin qu'il vous aide en lui demandant s'il *peut* le faire. Si vous ne lui demandez rien, vous n'obtiendrez rien de lui.

Lorsque vous demandez à votre homme de vous rendre service, comment réagit-il ? Répond-il à votre demande ?

« *Une fois sur deux, et c'est souvent parce que j'insiste. À force de le harceler, il finit par le faire pour avoir la paix.* »

Anabelle, 26 ans

« *Rarement. Je pense qu'il fait comme s'il n'avait pas entendu, qu'il sait que s'il ne fait pas ce que je lui demande, je vais finir par le faire moi-même.* »

Fanny, 32 ans

«Pas souvent. Quand je crie parce que je suis à bout de nerfs, il s'active un peu pour me donner un coup de main. Souvent, je ne lui laisse pas le choix. Par exemple, je me sauve et je le laisse seul avec les enfants.»

Christiane, 29 ans

«Il fait ce que je lui demande une fois sur deux. Il a tendance à oublier. Il m'avait promis que dès qu'il aurait son agenda électronique, il n'oublierait plus rien. Le problème, c'est que depuis qu'il l'a, il oublie d'y entrer ce qu'il a à faire. Ça a coûté 600 $ et je ne suis pas plus avancée!»

Solange, 37 ans

«Oui, parce que je joue la fille qui ne peut pas se passer de ses services. Et ça marche!»

Mariska, 41 ans

«Non, il ne me rend pas service souvent. J'ai même arrêté de lui demander certaines choses, ça nous évite bien des disputes.»

Angela, 24 ans

Règle n° 9

Passez du «tu» au «je»

Vous êtes la seule personne responsable de ce que vous ressentez. Vous ne pouvez pas tenir votre homme responsable de votre bonheur ou de votre malheur, et encore moins de *vos* réactions à ses comportements. Si votre homme est en retard, au lieu de lui balancer à la figure qu'il n'est pas fiable, qu'il ne vous respecte pas, qu'il est toujours en retard, etc., dites-lui que vous vous êtes inquiétée, que vous vous demandiez pourquoi il n'arrivait pas, etc. Vous ne pouvez pas supposer ce qu'il pense ou ce qu'il ressent, pas plus que vous ne pouvez savoir ce qui est réellement arrivé.

En utilisant le «je» au lieu du «tu», vous prenez la responsabilité de vos états d'âme et de vos émotions. En ne tenant pas votre homme responsable de ce que vous ressentez, vous lui démontrez du respect et il n'hésitera pas à s'expliquer clairement avec vous et à vous rassurer, car vous ne lui aurez pas fait de reproches. L'homme qui a déçu sa compagne fera tout ce qu'il peut pour se racheter. En agissant selon cette règle, vous avez le gros bout du bâton.

L'idée n'est pas d'excuser des comportements qui vous déplaisent pas mais de ne pas tenir votre homme responsable de ce que vous ressentez à cause d'eux. Vos émotions n'appartiennent qu'à vous seule. Si vous l'accablez de reproches chaque fois qu'il agit mal à vos yeux, il vous mentira ou vous donnera raison sur toute la ligne sans s'expliquer, et ce, juste pour avoir la paix, pour que vous vous taisiez enfin.

Si vous vous sentez incomprise, si vous trouvez votre conjoint ingrat, sans-cœur, dites-le-lui. Dites-lui surtout pourquoi vous vous sentez incomprise. Ne lui dites pas comment vous le trouvez, lui, mais plutôt comment *vous* vous sentez. Votre conjoint ne peut deviner vos sentiments, il n'est pas fait comme vous, il ne pense pas comme vous et n'accorde sûrement pas la même importance aux mêmes choses que vous.

Si vous lui dites quelle importance a quelque chose pour vous et pourquoi, il comprendra. Il n'est pas idiot, il a seulement besoin que vous le lui expliquiez.

Ne pas accuser l'autre ni s'autoaccuser est une façon simple de s'exprimer, d'être écoutée et d'écouter l'autre. Cette méthode demande de la pratique, mais les résultats sont surprenants.

Rappelez à votre homme que, lorsque vous lui parlez de vos problèmes, vous ne les lui reprochez pas, et que le simple fait de lui en parler vous fait le plus grand bien. Dites-lui que ce n'est pas sa faute, qu'il n'est pas responsable de tout ce que vous ressentez. Évidemment, vous ne devez pas ensuite le blâmer, le désapprouver, le critiquer ou chercher à le rabaisser. Utilisez le « je » le plus possible ; ce n'est pas toujours facile, mais cela vous évitera bien des disputes et des malentendus.

La règle du « je » est particulièrement importante lorsque vous exprimez vos sentiments. Si vous lui dites au « je » ce que vous ressentez, votre homme sera plus enclin à respecter vos sentiments et à les prendre en considération car il ne se sentira pas désapprouvé. Mais n'oubliez pas d'amener une chose à la fois, sans quoi vous pourriez le mêler. Et que fait l'homme quand il est mêlé ? Il se tait.

Si une femme exprime clairement ses besoins en utilisant le « je », son homme sera heureux de les combler. Lorsque vous demandez à votre homme de vous aider, faites-lui sentir que vous êtes convaincue qu'il y parviendra, que vous croyez qu'il peut le faire. Il est important de lui envoyer ce message, car ce que l'homme craint le plus, c'est de se révéler incompétent. S'il croit que vous pensez qu'il ne sera pas à la hauteur, il n'essaiera même pas. Il peut certes être difficile de lui faire faire ce que vous faites sans même qu'on vous l'ait demandé. Mais votre homme fonctionne selon un modèle différent du vôtre, et si vous savez vous y prendre, vos efforts ne seront pas vains et vous y trouverez votre compte.

Lorsque votre homme a fait quelque chose qui vous a déplu, comment lui en parlez-vous ?

————◄○►————

« *Je le lui dis sans passer par quatre chemins, ou je lui fais la gueule.* »

Anabelle, 26 ans

————◄○►————

« *Je ne le lui dis pas. Mon attitude le lui fait savoir assez clairement.* »

Fanny, 32 ans

————◄○►————

« *J'essaie de lui expliquer pourquoi ça m'a déplu, mais il se justifie aussitôt. Je le soupçonne d'inventer des excuses pour avoir la paix.* »

Christiane, 29 ans

————◄○►————

« *Je le traite de tous les noms avant de m'excuser et de lui dire pourquoi j'ai réagi aussi fort. Je sais qu'il trouve que j'ai des réactions exagérées par rapport à ses gaffes, mais l'accumulation de toutes les conneries qu'il fait finit par me mettre dans tous mes états.* »

Solange, 37 ans

————◄○►————

« Quand ça arrive, je lui dis que ça m'a fait de la peine, et il ne recommence plus. »

Mariska, 41 ans

―――――◦―――――

« Je lui dis clairement que je l'ai trouvé con, et on s'engueule. La plupart du temps, c'est moi qui ai le dernier mot. Et il ne recommence pas. Il a bien trop peur que je l'engueule de nouveau. »

Angela, 24 ans

―――――◦―――――

Règle n° 10

Donner moins = recevoir plus

Les femmes craignent de perdre quelque chose en arrêtant d'aider les autres. Les hommes craignent de perdre quelque chose en aidant les autres.

Les femmes font tout ce qu'elles peuvent pour que leur entourage soit bien, heureux, et ce, bien avant de se préoccuper de leur propre bien-être et de leur propre bonheur. Pour les hommes, c'est le contraire : ils se préoccupent de leur propre bien-être avant de se soucier de celui de leur entourage.

Parce qu'elles sentent que les autres ont besoin d'aide sans qu'ils aient eu à le demander, les femmes croient qu'elles n'ont pas non plus à demander de l'aide pour en recevoir, particulièrement de la part de leur conjoint. C'est une erreur : si vous ne demandez pas d'aide à votre homme, il ne vous l'offrira pas, car ce n'est pas dans sa nature.

Rappelez-vous, l'homme ne sait pas lire entre les lignes, il n'a pas de sixième sens pour deviner que celle qu'il aime a besoin d'aide. Il croit sincèrement que si sa femme ne lui demande pas son aide, c'est qu'elle n'en a pas besoin et qu'il en fait assez.

Dans un couple, il faut être présent, il faut appuyer l'autre, le soutenir, mais on ne peut pas faire les choses à sa place. Et si on décide de le faire, il ne faut rien attendre en retour, pas même de la reconnaissance. Ce n'est pas parce qu'on fait toute seule le ménage de la maison ou que l'on est seule à faire l'impossible pour respecter le budget que l'on doit attendre de son homme des remerciements ou un remboursement. Si vous décidez de faire quelque chose, faites-le, c'est tout. Vous ne pouvez demander à votre homme de vous donner en retour exactement ce que vous lui donnez, et de reconnaître votre générosité chaque fois que vous faites quelque chose pour lui. Il n'est ni égoïste ni désintéressé. Il ne voit pas les choses comme vous, voilà tout, et n'y accorde pas la même importance.

Bien des femmes se plaignent du fait que leur homme ne fait rien dans la maison. Mais lorsqu'ils se mettent enfin au travail, elles les blâment de ne pas le faire correctement, les engueulent et finissent par faire les choses elles-mêmes. Vu ce comportement, il n'est pas étonnant que tant d'hommes ne se risquent même pas à essayer de les aider, de peur de se faire « chicaner » et de prouver à leur compagne qu'ils sont incompétents.

Vous voulez que votre homme vous donne un coup de main, fasse des choses pour vous ? Laissez-le les faire à sa façon si vous voulez qu'il en prenne l'habitude. S'il ne s'y prend pas comme vous pour vider le lave-vaisselle ou pour donner le bain aux enfants, ça ne veut pas dire que ce n'est pas correct et que le résultat ne sera pas satisfaisant. L'important, c'est que ce soit fait. Vous ne pouvez pas exiger de votre homme – ni de qui que ce soit d'autre – qu'il fasse les choses exactement comme vous. Il n'a peut-être pas votre talent, mais si vous lui avez demandé de faire quelque chose, il croit que vous le savez capable de le faire. Le reprendre constamment pendant qu'il le fait, c'est lui dire tout à fait le contraire. Votre homme n'est pas un idiot. Sa façon de faire n'est peut-être pas la vôtre, mais au moins il fait quelque chose. N'était-ce pas cela que vous vouliez au départ ? Apprendre à déléguer, à être un peu moins perfectionniste et à ne pas donner trop d'importance aux petites choses du quotidien vous enlèvera un stress immense et vous permettra de passer plus de temps, et du temps de qualité, avec celui que vous aimez.

Tout n'est pas une question de vie ou de mort. Ce n'est pas grave si le ménage n'est pas parfait, si la vaisselle n'est pas faite immédiatement après le repas, si votre homme a oublié de passer chercher du pain en rentrant du travail, etc. Ne jouez pas à la *drama queen* ! Un homme qui vit sous un régime de terreur cessera toute activité susceptible de faire fâcher sa compagne. Plutôt que de subir des reproches et d'écouter le récit des drames de sa femme, l'homme préférera s'impliquer le moins possible et s'éloignera petit à petit pour éviter les foudres.

L'homme a tendance à accorder du temps et de l'énergie aux choses importantes et à minimiser les petites et les détails qu'il juge moins importants. La femme doit donc voir les petits oublis de son homme comme des détails qu'il a écartés parce qu'il ne les jugeait pas assez importants.

Cela n'a rien à voir avec l'amour qu'il éprouve pour sa partenaire. C'est tout simplement sa façon de penser qui est différente. L'homme n'agit pas d'abord en fonction des autres, mais en fonction de son propre bien-être. Ce n'est pas de l'égoïsme, c'est tout simplement qu'il est ainsi. Sa nature est ainsi faite. Bien des femmes pourraient d'ailleurs s'inspirer du comportement des hommes dans ce domaine. Cela leur éviterait bien du stress et des angoisses.

Exprimez à votre homme, clairement et de façon concise, ce que vous voudriez qu'il fasse pour que vous vous sentiez bien. N'exigez rien de lui ; demandez-lui plutôt s'il *peut* le faire, car cela vous aiderait et vous ferait du bien. S'il se sent indispensable, votre homme pourra soulever des montagnes, mais si vous ne lui demandez rien, il croira qu'il en fait assez ou que vous n'avez pas besoin de lui. Si vous êtes seule à faire toutes les corvées de la maison et que vous continuez de les faire sans lui demander s'il peut vous aider, ne lui reprochez pas de ne rien faire. Il ne peut deviner que vous avez besoin d'aide à moins que vous ne le lui disiez clairement, car c'est un homme et que les hommes ne voient pas ces choses-là.

L'homme ne sait aucunement que sa compagne a besoin de lui tant et aussi longtemps qu'elle ne le lui aura pas dit clairement. Demandez-lui de l'aide dès que vous en avez besoin ; demandez-lui s'il peut faire telle ou telle chose pour vous. N'attendez pas des siècles pour le faire, car alors vous exploserez et lui balancerez une tonne de reproches à la figure. Et si vous agissez ainsi, vous n'obtiendrez rien de lui.

Lorsqu'une femme prend la décision de moins donner à son homme afin de recevoir davantage de lui, elle croit qu'elle sera jugée, rejetée, moins appréciée, voire abandonnée. Pourtant, elle aussi a le droit de recevoir davantage, et si l'homme se heurte à des refus ou à des barrières, il verra là un défi qu'il ne pourra s'empêcher de relever. Après tout, c'est un héros !

Donc, demandez plus d'aide à votre homme et soyez moins exigeante envers vous-même. C'est là le plus beau cadeau que vous puissiez lui offrir et vous offrir.

Croyez-vous en faire plus pour votre homme qu'il n'en fait pour vous ?

« *Oui, c'est sûr. Si c'était juste de mon chum, on vivrait dans un taudis insalubre et on n'aurait que du linge sale à se mettre sur le dos. Il n'est pas terrible dans une maison, et quand je le laisse faire, c'est souvent à recommencer. Aussi bien me débrouiller toute seule que de réparer ses dégâts.* »

Anabelle, 26 ans

«*Absolument! Mon chum ne fait rien dans la maison, il ne fait jamais l'épicerie et ne va jamais chercher les enfants à la garderie. On travaille tous les deux, mais j'accomplis toutes les tâches dans la maison.*»

Fanny, 32 ans

«*J'en fais plus que lui, c'est certain. On dirait qu'il est aveugle et qu'il ne voit pas ce qu'il y a à faire. Quand je lui demande quelque chose, il oublie aussitôt. Je crois que je l'ai trop gâté au départ et qu'il tient pour acquis tout ce que je fais pour lui.*»

Solange, 37 ans

«*Je fais tout le ménage, toutes les courses, je m'occupe des enfants, je me tape les devoirs, le lavage, les repas, lui, il tond le gazon l'été et déneige la cour l'hiver, pas parce qu'il veut me faire plaisir, mais parce qu'il refuse que je touche à sa tondeuse et à sa souffleuse.*»

Christiane, 29 ans

«*Pas vraiment. Avec les années (ça fait 20 ans qu'on est ensemble), on a appris à séparer les tâches. Je m'occupe des trucs dans lesquels il n'excelle pas vraiment et il fait ceux que je n'aime pas faire. Quand il ne fait pas sa part, je ne la fais pas pour lui. Ça doit être ça, la sagesse...*»

Mariska, 41 ans

« Oui, parce que quand je le laisse faire le ménage, par exemple, c'est pire que s'il ne l'avait pas fait. Il est vraiment nul pour tout ce qui touche à la maison, et je n'ai vraiment pas la patience de lui apprendre à bien faire les choses. »

Angela, 24 ans

Règle nº 11

Pas de conseils!

Ne donnez pas de conseils à votre homme, à moins qu'il ne vous le demande. Vouloir aider votre homme en lui disant quoi faire provient certainement d'une bonne intention, mais pour lui, c'est une insulte. En l'inondant de conseils et de directives, vous lui envoyez le message qu'il est incompétent, dépendant, et que vous le croyez incapable de régler ses problèmes tout seul. Et même si ce n'est pas du tout ce que vous croyez, lui le croira.

L'homme juge primordial de s'occuper seul de ses affaires, de régler lui-même ses problèmes, comme un grand garçon. Si sa compagne lui dit toujours comment s'occuper des détails de la vie courante, il sera convaincu qu'elle ne lui fait pas confiance pour les choses plus importantes. Il ne s'en occupera donc pas plus, et vous trouverez qu'il n'en fait pas assez pour vous soutenir. Admirez votre homme et aimez-le pour ce qu'il fait de bien plutôt que de critiquer ce qu'il fait de mal et de lui dire quoi faire.

Laissez votre homme se tromper sans lui mettre sous le nez que vous l'aviez prévenu ; de toute façon, il s'en souvient très bien. Au lieu de vous attarder à ses échecs, appréciez ses réussites et soulignez-les. Plus on accable un homme, plus on sème la certitude qu'on ne le croit pas capable de faire quelque chose de bien. Et alors, il ne fera plus rien.

Dites à votre homme que vous l'aimez tel qu'il est et que ce n'est pas grave si, par exemple, il ne sait pas faire la cuisine, car c'est un homme exceptionnel et que vous avez besoin de lui. Après cela, votre homme multipliera les efforts pour vous prouver que vous avez raison. Qui sait ? Il se mettra peut-être même à cuisiner ! Si vous persuadez votre homme qu'il est votre héros, il fera tout ce qu'il peut pour vous combler et vous prouver que vous avez raison.

Si vous essayez d'aider votre homme sans qu'il ait sollicité votre aide, il pourrait croire que vous tentez de le manipuler ou de l'amener à changer. Soutenir son homme, c'est l'aimer en cessant de le critiquer ou de remettre en question ses qualités ou ses capacités.

Si vous voulez absolument lui donner un conseil, mettez-vous à sa place et réfléchissez un moment à ce que vous feriez à sa place. Dites-lui ensuite, après avoir formulé votre conseil, ce que vous feriez si vous vous trouviez dans une telle situation. Dites-lui que cela vous inquiète un peu de le voir dans cette situation, mais que vous êtes persuadée qu'il s'en sortira, comme il l'a toujours fait. En faisant cela, vous donnez votre avis sans lui imposer votre point de vue ni lui dire quoi faire. Vous partagez vos émotions sans les lui imposer. Si vous agissez ainsi, il ne serait pas étonnant que votre homme vous demande de l'aider, simplement parce qu'il a le choix et sait qu'il peut vous faire confiance. Et n'allez pas croire que c'est là de la manipulation ; il s'agit plutôt de savoir jouer les cartes de votre jeu en lui laissant le choix d'entamer la partie seul ou avec vous.

Quand vous voulez aider votre homme, avec ou sans son accord, comment réagit-il ?

« *Je lui donne mon avis et je lui laisse le choix d'en tenir compte ou pas. Mais s'il n'en tient pas compte et qu'il manque son coup, je me fais un plaisir de le lui rappeler.* »

Anabelle, 26 ans

« *Il réagit très mal. Il détruit tous mes conseils à coup d'arguments plus ou moins valables et finit toujours par n'en faire qu'à sa tête, ce qui n'est pas toujours très heureux…* »

Fanny, 32 ans

« *Je ne lui donne pas de conseils, je lui dis quoi faire et, s'il ne le fait pas, c'est son problème, pas le mien.* »

Christiane, 29 ans

« J'essaie de ne pas me mêler de ses affaires, mais quand ça concerne la maison, les enfants ou notre couple, je lui suggère fortement de m'écouter et de faire ce que je lui dis. Il ne reconnaît jamais que j'ai de bonnes idées pour résoudre nos ennuis, mais il sait que s'il fait ce que je lui ai dit de faire, il les réglera. »

Solange, 37 ans

« Pour ça, je suis un peu ratoureuse. Je lui donne des conseils mais en lui faisant croire que ça vient de lui. Ça marche à tout coup. Je ne peux pas croire qu'après toutes ces années il ne s'est pas rendu compte de mon petit manège. »

Mariska, 41 ans

« Qu'il le veuille ou non, je dois absolument conseiller et aider mon chum, sans cela il ne sortirait jamais des situations impossibles dans lesquelles il se met. Avant moi, c'est sa mère qui s'occupait de lui comme ça. Ça vous donne une idée de son peu de maturité. »

Angela, 24 ans

Règle n° 12

Le droit à l'erreur

Quand l'homme commet une erreur, il a de la difficulté à s'excuser car il croit que sa partenaire ne lui pardonnera jamais. Inconsciemment ou non, les femmes ont tendance à exprimer leur désapprobation, donnant à l'homme une raison de plus de ne pas s'excuser. Lorsqu'il a commis une erreur, l'homme devient très sensible et vulnérable, il est alors facile pour la femme de l'écraser, car il se sent déjà assez à terre.

Lorsque votre homme commet une erreur, abstenez-vous de tout commentaire. S'il vous a déçu, il le sait et tentera de se justifier en vous expliquant pourquoi vous ne devriez pas être déçue ni bouleversée. Il est clair que vous ne voulez pas le savoir, que vous voulez seulement qu'il vous écoute. Dites-le-lui et dites-lui aussi que ce n'est pas grave s'il se soit trompé, qu'il n'en a pas moins de valeur à vos yeux et que vous l'aimez tout autant. Après cela, il s'excusera sincèrement et sera prêt à vous écouter s'il sait que cela peut vous aider à oublier sa bévue.

Il y a aussi des hommes qui se fâchent lorsqu'ils commettent une erreur. Ils ne l'acceptent pas et ne veulent pas vous entendre. Rassurez-vous, ils n'en ont pas après vous, c'est à eux-mêmes qu'ils en veulent. Quand votre homme se met à crier, il n'y a qu'une chose à faire : partez et laissez-le tout seul. Allez-vous-en sans rien dire et attendez que la tempête passe. Si vous essayez d'échanger avec lui lorsqu'il est en colère, vous ne ferez qu'empirer les choses. Attendez qu'il se calme avant de lui parler. Une fois la crise passée, faites-lui comprendre que vous ne le désapprouvez pas et que vous ne l'aimez pas moins. Dites-vous que sa colère n'est pas due à la bêtise qu'il a commise mais à ce que vous pouvez penser de lui.

On l'a dit, les hommes ont besoin d'être rassurés en ce qui a trait à leurs compétences et à leurs capacités, et c'est lorsqu'ils commettent une erreur ou ont fait quelque chose qui a blessé leur partenaire qu'ils en ont le plus besoin.

Laissez-le faire ses erreurs, laissez-le se tromper sans lui mettre ses bévues sous le nez. De cette façon, il apprendra et, qui sait, la prochaine fois, peut-être vous demandera-t-il votre aide parce qu'il saura – vous le lui aurez prouvé en le laissant se tromper sans lui faire de reproches – que vous lui faites confiance.

Quand votre homme commet une erreur, comment réagissez-vous ?

------------◦------------

« Je lui dis simplement qu'il s'est trompé et je le laisse se débrouiller avec les conséquences de son erreur. »

Anabelle, 26 ans

------------◦------------

« Je lui dis que ce n'est pas très surprenant et j'essaie, si je le peux, d'arranger les choses. »

Fanny, 32 ans

------------◦------------

« Maintenant, je n'en parle pas très longtemps. Je l'engueule un peu et je passe à autre chose, le laissant se sortir tout seul du bourbier dans lequel il s'est mis. »

Solange, 37 ans

------------◦------------

« Je l'engueule, parce que ça lui arrive souvent. Je me dis, comme pour un enfant, qu'il va finir par apprendre. »

Christiane, 29 ans

------------◦------------

« Je ne lui dis rien. C'est le meilleur moyen que j'ai trouvé pour qu'il ne recommence pas. Il sait qu'il a gaffé, je n'ai pas besoin de le lui rappeler. Ne rien lui dire le force à arranger les choses et à s'excuser. »

Mariska, 41 ans

------------◦------------

«*Je lui dis de ne plus recommencer, que c'est arrivé parce qu'il ne m'a pas écoutée, et je lui dis quoi faire pour se sortir de là. Je suis sûre que ce serait moins difficile d'élever un enfant que de m'occuper de mon chum.*»

Angela, 24 ans

Règle nº 13

«Get a life!»

Admettez que votre homme a besoin de liberté. Lui accorder trop d'attention, jouer à la mère avec lui, vouloir être toujours avec lui, c'est étouffer la nature même de l'homme que vous aimez.

Votre homme cherche à être indépendant, à fonctionner par lui-même, et il voudrait que vous fassiez de même. Autant il souhaite que vous ayez besoin de lui et qu'il vous soit indispensable, autant il craint de ne jamais avoir de moments à lui seul si vous en venez à ne pas avoir d'autres centres d'intérêt que lui dans la vie.

Si vous avez des activités, si vous suivez des cours, si vous voyez vos amis, votre homme sera heureux pour vous. Et, enfin, il pourra avoir des moments à lui, moments qui sont si importants à son bien-être. Vous voir vivre des choses sans lui rend votre homme heureux. Et il sera si content de vous retrouver ensuite !

Si votre homme est votre seul centre d'intérêt, il est grand temps que vous fassiez quelque chose pour remédier à la situation. Sans cela, vous mettez votre couple en danger.

Votre homme ne doit pas être la seule personne à qui vous pouvez parler. Confiez-vous à vos amies, à votre sœur, à votre mère. Ne mettez pas tout le poids de votre bonheur sur les épaules de votre homme. Cette responsabilité vous revient d'abord à vous. Si vous n'êtes pas heureuse, ne comptez pas sur votre homme pour vous apporter le bonheur. Il peut faire beaucoup de choses pour vous, mais c'est à vous que cela revient, de la même façon que vous n'êtes pas non plus responsable de son bonheur ou de son malheur.

Vous aviez une vie avant de tomber amoureuse de votre homme? Elle ne doit pas disparaître! Vous n'êtes pas seulement la compagne de Monsieur, vous êtes aussi, et surtout, une personne à part entière, avec des activités et des intérêts qui vous sont propres. Vous n'avez pas besoin de votre homme pour faire ce que vous voulez. Sinon, comment auriez-vous fait pour vivre avant de le rencontrer?

Autant votre homme a besoin de se sentir indispensable à vos yeux, autant il ne peut supporter que vous comptiez sur lui pour vivre votre vie, sans lui laisser le choix. Lorsque vous concentrez toute votre énergie et tout votre intérêt sur votre conjoint, il se sent rapidement coincé car il sait que vous ne ferez rien s'il n'est pas là. Lui, tout ce qu'il souhaite, c'est d'être seul quelquefois tout en sachant que vous êtes bien et que vous vous occupez à autre chose qu'à vous inquiéter de lui.

De la même façon, lorsqu'il a besoin de silence pour réfléchir, il est important qu'il sache que vous êtes occupée et que vous ne vous souciez pas de lui car vous avez autre chose à faire.

La solitude est bonne pour les deux personnes du couple. Quand les conjoints sont capables de passer du temps l'un sans l'autre sans en faire tout un plat, les moments où ils se retrouvent ensemble sont plus agréables, plus constructifs, et ils donnent au couple les moments d'intimité dont il a besoin pour survivre. C'est quand on s'ennuie, au moins un peu, de son partenaire, qu'on a le plus hâte d'être avec lui.

Avez-vous besoin d'être souvent avec votre conjoint ? Comment vous sentez-vous quand vous n'êtes pas avec lui ?

« *Quand mon chum n'est pas avec moi, je me demande toujours ce qu'il fait et avec qui. Comme il ne me dit jamais rien, je m'inquiète et, quand il rentre à la maison, j'essaie de savoir ce qu'il a fait.* »

Anabelle, 26 ans

« Enfin, j'ai la paix ! Cela dit, j'aime savoir où il se trouve et ce qu'il fait quand il n'est pas avec moi. »

Fanny, 32 ans

————◦————

« Ça ne me fait ni chaud ni froid, du moment que je sais où il est. »

Solange, 37 ans

————◦————

« J'aime passer du temps avec mon chum. Mais plus je lui demande de rester avec moi, plus il a envie de sortir. »

Christiane, 29 ans

————◦————

« Ça ne me fait rien. Je suis tellement occupée de mon côté que ce serait égoïste de ma part d'exiger qu'il soit toujours disponible quand moi je ne le suis pas. »

Mariska, 41 ans

————◦————

« Je veux passer le plus de temps possible avec lui, parce que je l'aime et qu'il m'aime. Quand on s'aime, on doit passer le plus de temps possible ensemble pour en profiter. »

Angela, 24 ans

————◦————

Règle nº 14

À ne pas faire...

On l'a déjà dit, l'homme est délicat, sensible, et il y a des choses qu'il vaut mieux éviter de faire ou de dire pour ne pas le voir se refermer et s'éloigner de soi.

Par exemple, une chose qui ne manquera pas de provoquer les pires réactions chez votre homme, c'est de le reprendre en public. C'est le pire des affronts, car alors non seulement vous remettez en question ses capacités et ses compétences, mais vous le faites devant témoins, comme si vous vouliez leur prouver à eux aussi qu'il est un incapable et un incompétent. Pour l'homme, ce genre de comportement de la part de sa partenaire est très dur à digérer.

Il vaut mieux ne jamais reprendre, et encore moins réprimander, votre homme en public, que ce soit devant la famille, les enfants, les collègues ou les amis. Si votre homme fait des gestes ou a une attitude que vous n'approuvez pas ou que vous n'aimez pas, attendez d'être dans la voiture ou à la maison pour le lui dire. Lorsqu'il y a des gens autour de vous, ce n'est pas le moment d'entamer une telle discussion. Et si ce qu'il fait vous choque, raison de plus pour attendre d'être seule avec lui pour lui en parler : il n'est jamais bon de parler sous le coup de la colère.

Lorsque vous vous retrouvez seule avec lui et que la poussière est retombée, dites-lui (en utilisant le «je») que vous n'avez pas aimé ce qu'il a dit ou la façon dont il a agi, que cela vous a mise mal à l'aise et que vous aimeriez qu'il ne le fasse plus, du moins en votre présence. Il est fort probable qu'il s'excusera et qu'il ne recommencera pas, du moins avec vous.

Deuxièmement, veillez à ne jamais taquiner votre homme en faisant des blagues ou en passant des commentaires sur ses cheveux, sa taille et ses habiletés manuelles. Même si c'était juste pour rire, il verrait là une critique très personnelle et blessante de votre part, un jugement sur sa valeur. Imaginez l'inverse : votre homme se moquerait gentiment de vos bourrelets, de vos seins ou de vos talents de ménagère. Vous le prendriez de travers, n'est-ce pas? Vous vous mettriez rapidement à douter de son attirance pour vous, de son amour, etc. Eh bien, c'est la même chose pour votre homme, qui est aussi sensible que vous. Toutefois, il ne l'exprimerait pas par des mots mais vous éviterait pour ne pas vous décevoir encore plus. Ne vous aventurez donc pas sur ce terrain : c'est une zone minée.

Troisièmement, il y a des sujets à éviter. Par exemple, évitez de lui dire à quel point vous admirez d'autres hommes de votre entourage. Il prendrait cela comme une critique à son endroit et verrait là un moyen détourné de lui faire comprendre qu'il ne vous satisfait pas et que vous ne le trouvez pas à la hauteur. Il croirait que vous le faites exprès et même que vous tentez de le manipuler pour lui faire faire ce que vous voulez.

Enfin, si vous voulez qu'il vous écoute avec attention, n'allez surtout pas lui parler…

- des prouesses de votre animal de compagnie ;
- des aventures de vos vedettes préférées ;
- des intrigues de vos émissions préférées ;
- de vos séances de magasinage ;
- des problèmes et des angoisses de vos copines ;
- de ce dont vous avez discuté avec une amie ;
- des médecines douces et des produits naturels ;
- de vos problèmes féminins.

Ce genre de sujets le met très mal à l'aise parce qu'il n'a aucune idée de ce dont vous lui parlez et des raisons pour lesquelles vous lui dites tout cela.

Les règles en bref

Règle n° 1   L'homme réfléchit en silence

- Il a besoin de s'isoler pour mieux comprendre ce que vous venez de lui dire.

- Il doit réfléchir dans le calme pour mettre de l'ordre dans ses idées avant de les exprimer.

- Il a besoin de ces moments de silence pour communiquer avec vous.

- Il a besoin de s'isoler pour trouver le besoin de vivre des moments d'intimité avec vous.

- S'il s'éloigne, ce n'est pas parce qu'il ne s'intéresse pas à ce que vous dites mais parce qu'il en a besoin.

- N'insistez jamais pour que votre homme vous parle s'il n'a pas pris le temps de réfléchir, il ne vous dira rien parce qu'il ne trouvera rien à vous dire.

Règle n° 2   Soyez claire et concise

–   Posez des questions claires, courtes et précises pour avoir une réponse digne de ce nom.

–   Ne comptez pas sur lui pour deviner l'intention derrière vos propos ; si vous ne lui précisez pas, il ne pourra le savoir.

–   L'homme n'est pas aussi sensible et clairvoyant que la femme, il ne sait pas ce dont les autres ont besoin.

–   L'homme ne sait pas lire entre les lignes, il ne décode pas les non-dits.

–   Chaque fois que vous posez une question à votre homme, précisez-lui dès le départ le but de votre question, votre intention et en quoi sa réponse vous sera utile.

Règle n° 3   L'homme parle si c'est utile

–   L'homme n'aime pas parler seulement pour le plaisir ; il doit toujours y avoir une raison ou un motif.

–   Prenez l'initiative de la conversation.

–   S'il se sent utile, s'il sent qu'il peut faire quelque chose pour vous, il sera heureux de vous écouter et même de vous parler.

–   S'il n'y a pas de raison valable de parler aux yeux de votre homme, plus vous tenterez de l'y forcer, plus il se réfugiera dans le silence, jusqu'à éviter tout échange avec vous.

–   Quand vous lui parlez de vos problèmes, votre homme croit que vous les lui reprochez ou que vous lui demandez de l'aide ; dans les deux cas, il voudra vous aider en vous bombardant de solutions.

- Si vous voulez seulement qu'il vous écoute, dites-le-lui dès le début.

- Pour s'ouvrir à vous, votre homme doit sentir que vous lui faites confiance.

Règle n° 4   Un problème = une solution

- Pour l'homme, l'émotion exprime un problème ou un conflit.

- Si vous lui parlez de vos problèmes, il voudra absolument trouver une solution pour vous aider, parce qu'il se sent responsable des problèmes.

- L'homme ne parle pas de ses problèmes à sa compagne, car il veut absolument les régler seul.

- Pour se faire du bien, l'homme a besoin de s'isoler pour trouver des solutions et agir.

- Si l'homme a des problèmes, il n'en parlera pas à sa partenaire, de peur qu'elle le juge incompétent.

- L'homme ne s'occupe que des choses qu'il juge importantes.

- L'homme préfère l'action à la discussion.

- Confiez vos petits ennuis à vos copines plutôt qu'à votre conjoint, du moins si ça ne le concerne pas.

Règle n° 5   Acceptez ses réponses

- Si vous posez une question à votre homme, acceptez ses réponses, quelles qu'elles soient.

– Si vous voulez seulement qu'il vous approuve et vous réconforte, dites-le-lui dès le départ.

– Dès qu'il vous propose une solution, l'homme croit que le problème est réglé et que la discussion est terminée.

– Ne vous servez pas des confidences faites dans le passé pour gagner un point ou lui prouver que vous avez raison.

– L'homme est plus cérébral que la femme, et celle-ci est plus émotive que lui. C'est pourquoi il tente de vous raisonner lorsque vous lui parlez; il veut comprendre.

– Si vous ne voulez pas qu'il vous donne des conseils, dites-le-lui dès le départ. Sinon, il ne vous donnera que ça.

Règle n° 6 Laissez-le parler sans l'accuser de le faire !

– Lorsque votre homme vous parle, laissez-le terminer ce qu'il a à vous dire sans l'interrompre. Si vous lui coupez la parole en lui apportant des éléments nouveaux ou lui faisant part de votre désapprobation, il sera mêlé et plongera dans le silence pour réfléchir et absorber l'information.

– Laissez-le parler jusqu'au bout, puis demandez-lui s'il a bien terminé. Résumez ensuite ce qu'il vous a dit pour vous assurer que vous avez bien compris.

– S'il n'a pas répondu à votre question, laissez-le tout de même terminer avant de reformuler votre question ou de lui demander de préciser sa pensée.

– Ne lui reprochez pas de répondre autre chose que ce que vous vouliez entendre. Ce n'est pas vous qui devez parler à travers lui, c'est lui qui vous parle.

– Écoutez votre homme attentivement, en l'encourageant à continuer, et, avec le temps, il vous parlera sans que vous le lui ayez demandé.

Règle nᵒ 7   Ne répondez pas à sa place

– Quand vous répondez à la place de votre homme, vous lui dites que vous ne le trouvez pas assez bien pour le faire lui-même.

– Répondre à sa place, c'est rejeter sa réponse et, pour lui, cela équivaut à être rejeté.

– S'il vous demande de l'aider parce qu'il ne sait pas quoi dire, répondez comme vous croyez qu'il le ferait, et vérifiez avec lui si c'est bien cela qu'il aurait dit.

Règle nᵒ 8   Passez du vouloir au pouvoir

– Demandez-lui s'il *peut* faire quelque chose pour vous, et non s'il *veut* faire quelque chose pour vous.

– Demandez quelque chose à votre homme au lieu de l'exiger de lui.

– Faites appel à ses compétences. S'il se sent utile, il pourra déplacer des montagnes pour vous.

– L'homme a besoin de savoir que vous l'admirez et que vous avez besoin de lui.

– Chaque fois que vous lui demandez quelque chose, soyez prête à essuyer un refus.

–   Lorsque votre homme refuse de vous aider, acceptez son refus simplement, sans drame.

–   Si vous ne demandez rien à votre homme, il sera convaincu qu'il en fait suffisamment pour vous.

Règle n° 9   Passez du «tu» au «je»

–   Vous êtes responsable de ce que vous ressentez.

–   Lorsque vous parlez à votre homme, faites-le le plus possible en utilisant le «je»; vous éviterez ainsi de l'accuser ou de l'insulter inutilement.

–   Un homme qui a déçu sa compagne fera tout pour se racheter.

–   Pour exprimer vos sentiments, utilisez le «je», c'est très important. Votre homme aura plus de respect pour ce que vous ressentez si vous lui dites avec le «je» et que vous exprimez votre point de vue à vous.

Règle n° 10 Donner moins = recevoir plus

–   L'homme croit sincèrement que si sa femme ne lui demande pas d'aide, c'est qu'elle n'en a pas besoin.

–   Refuser de faire des choses pour votre homme, c'est lui lancer un défi, et il ne peut résister à un défi. Après tout, c'est un héros!

–   L'homme pense à son bien-être avant de penser à celui des autres.

–   Quand votre homme se décide enfin à faire des choses pour vous, laissez-le les faire à sa façon.

- Apprenez à déléguer, à être moins perfectionniste et à accepter que les choses peuvent être faites, et bien faites, de plusieurs façons.

- Votre homme oublie souvent des choses parce qu'il ne peut penser à plus d'une chose à la fois et qu'il n'accorde pas la même importance que vous aux mêmes choses.

Règle n° 11 Pas de conseils !

- Ne donnez pas de conseil à votre homme, à moins qu'il ne vous le demande.

- Le conseiller ou lui dire quoi faire, c'est lui dire qu'il est incompétent et qu'il est incapable de faire quelque chose.

- Admirez votre homme et aimez-le pour ce qu'il fait de bien au lieu de le critiquer au sujet de ce qu'il ne réussit pas et de lui dire quoi faire.

- L'homme qui se fait aider contre son gré se sent manipulé et craint que l'on veuille le transformer.

- Rassurez-le en lui disant que vous lui faites confiance et que vous savez qu'il s'en sortira.

Règle n° 12 Le droit à l'erreur

- L'homme a de la difficulté à admettre qu'il a commis une erreur. Pour lui, cela revient à avouer son incompétence.

- Lorsqu'il se trompe, l'homme est très sensible et très vulnérable, ce n'est donc pas le moment de l'attaquer à grands coups de reproches.

- S'il vous a déçu, dites-lui, en utilisant le «je», comment vous vous sentez. Il vous écoutera et fera tout ce qu'il faut pour réparer sa bévue.

- Quand votre homme est en colère, laissez-le tranquille et attendez que la tempête soit finie pour lui parler.

- Ne lui mettez pas ses erreurs sous le nez. Il sait qu'il s'est trompé, il n'a pas besoin de vous pour le lui rappeler.

Règle n° 13 *«Get a life!»*

- Votre homme a besoin de liberté et il se sent libre quand il sait que vous pouvez avoir des activités sans lui.

- Votre homme ne doit pas être votre seul centre d'intérêt ni la seule personne à qui vous parlez.

- Vous n'êtes pas seulement la compagne de votre homme. Vous devez être une personne à part entière, avec ses activités et ses intérêts propres.

- Passez du temps seule, comme votre homme le fait, en vous occupant sans vous inquiéter de lui. Vos moments ensemble seront ainsi plus agréables et plus constructifs pour votre couple.

Règle n° 14 À ne pas faire...

- Ne reprenez jamais votre homme en public.

- N'agacez jamais votre homme en faisant des blagues ou en passant des commentaires sur ses cheveux, sa taille ou ses habiletés manuelles.

- Ne lui dites pas à quel point vous admirez d'autres hommes.

- Les sujets qui intéressent vos copines ne l'intéressent pas, évitez donc de lui en parler.

En terminant, sachez que toutes ces règles, même si elles vous demandent un effort, seront profitables non seulement pour vous, mais aussi pour la santé de votre couple. Non seulement vous arriverez ainsi à faire parler votre homme, mais vous parviendrez à mieux le comprendre et, surtout, à vous faire mieux comprendre vous-même.

Quand la femme sait comment l'homme fonctionne, il est plus facile pour elle de lui faire comprendre, si elle a les outils pour le faire, comment elle fonctionne elle-même. Ainsi, elle verra enfin ses besoins comblés par l'homme qu'elle aime.

Les règles pour faire parler votre homme sont efficaces parce qu'elles respectent les différences qui existent entre l'homme et la femme au sein du couple. De plus, ces règles ne font pas appel à la manipulation, au chantage ou à une quelconque soumission de votre part. Certes, cela vous demandera des efforts, mais c'est vous, en premier lieu, qui en récolterez les fruits, et votre couple ne s'en portera que mieux.

Pour que son couple fonctionne bien, la femme doit comprendre qu'elle n'est jamais si bien servie que par elle-même. Lorsqu'elle veut une chose, Dieu le veut aussi et c'est l'homme qui la lui obtient.

Le test
des trois passoires

Socrate avait, dans la Grèce antique, une haute réputation de sagesse. Quelqu'un vint un jour trouver le grand philosophe et lui dit :

— Sais-tu ce que je viens d'apprendre sur ton ami ?

— Un instant, répondit Socrate, avant que tu me racontes, j'aimerais te faire passer un test, celui des trois passoires.

— Les trois passoires ?

— Mais oui, reprit Socrate, avant de raconter toutes sortes de choses sur les autres, il est bon de prendre le temps de filtrer ce que l'on aimerait dire. C'est ce que j'appelle le test des trois passoires. La première passoire est celle de la vérité. As-tu vérifié si ce que tu veux dire est vrai ?

– Non, j'en ai seulement entendu parler...

– Très bien. Tu ne sais donc pas si c'est la vérité. Essayons de filtrer autrement en utilisant une deuxième passoire, celle de la bonté. Ce que tu veux m'apprendre sur mon ami, est-ce quelque chose de bien?

– Ah non! Au contraire!

– Donc, continua Socrate, tu veux me raconter de mauvaises choses sur lui et tu n'es même pas sûr qu'elles sont vraies. Tu peux peut-être encore passer le test, car il reste une passoire, celle de l'utilité. Est-il utile que tu m'apprennes ce que mon ami aurait fait?

– Pas vraiment.

– Alors, conclut Socrate, si ce que tu as à me raconter n'est ni vrai, ni bien, ni utile, pourquoi vouloir me le dire?

Auteur inconnu

Ils ont dit...

« Rien n'est plus doux au cœur d'un homme que le ravissement de la femme qu'il aime, qui l'aime, et la mine attentive qu'elle prend à chacune de ses paroles, d'autant plus émue et intérieurement grisée qu'elle ne sait pas ce qu'il lui dit. »

Jules Renard, écrivain français

———◇———

« Dialogue de couple.
Elle : Je me sens si seule !
Lui : Moi, pas assez. »

Jean Dutourd, romancier français

———◇———

« Les hommes parlent aux femmes pour pouvoir coucher avec elles ; les femmes couchent avec les hommes pour pouvoir parler avec eux. »

Jay McInerny, romancier américain

———◇———

« Lorsque les femmes ne vivront pas seulement à travers leur mari ou leurs enfants, les hommes n'auront plus peur de l'amour ni de la force des femmes et n'auront plus besoin de la faiblesse de l'autre pour être sûrs de leur propre masculinité. »

Betty Friedan, écrivaine

———◦———

« Quand quatre hommes ou plus se rencontrent, ils parlent de sport. Quand quatre femmes ou plus se rencontrent, elles parlent des hommes. »

Rita Rudner, humoriste américaine

———◦———

« C'est dur de faire un couple. Ça prend une vie. »

Hélène Ségara, chanteuse

———◦———

« Il n'y a pas de femme au monde qui puisse résister aux soins assidus et à toutes les attentions d'un homme qui veut la rendre amoureuse. »

Giovanni Casanova, écrivain et séducteur italien

———◦———

« Le plus beau cadeau que puisse offrir une femme à un homme, c'est la tranquillité. »

Helen Fielding, journaliste et romancière anglaise

———◦———

«Pour bâtir un couple, il faut être quatre : un homme plus sa part de féminité, une femme plus sa part de virilité.»

Bernard Werber, écrivain français

———◄○►———

« Si vous enseignez à un homme, vous enseignez à une personne. Si vous enseignez à une femme, vous enseignez à toute la famille.»

Proverbe indien

———◄○►———

«Les hommes ont confiance en eux, car ils grandissent en s'identifiant à des super-héros. Les femmes ont une mauvaise image d'elles-mêmes, car elles grandissent en s'identifiant à Barbie.»

Rita Rudner, humoriste américaine

———◄○►———

«Dans un couple, c'est l'homme qui décide, mais c'est la femme qui choisit.»

Anonyme

———◄○►———

«Les femmes ne veulent pas être les égales des hommes. Il faudrait nous lobotomiser pour ça !»

Roseanne Barr, actrice américaine

———◄○►———

« Il ne faut pas céder à l'impulsion : il faut, au contraire, la plier au devoir de chaque instant. C'est indispensable à l'harmonie du couple. »

Roland Lorrain, romancier québécois

———◦———

« Après l'amour, l'homme s'endort, alors que la femme pense. »

Monica Bellucci, actrice italienne

———◦———

« Dans un couple, peut-être que l'important n'est pas de vouloir rendre l'autre heureux, mais plutôt de se rendre heureux et d'offrir ce bonheur à l'autre. »

Jacques Salomé, psychologue français

———◦———

« Les hommes n'aiment pas les femmes spirituelles. Ils ont peur de ne pas être à la hauteur. »

Yvan Audouard, journaliste et romancier français

———◦———

« La chose la plus importante en communication, c'est d'entendre ce qui n'est pas dit. »

Peter Drucker, théoricien du marketing américain

———◦———

« Former un couple, c'est n'être qu'un ; mais lequel ? »

Proverbe anglais

———◦———

Table des matières